If You're Not a Celebrity … You're a Commodity!

How to Use the SECRET OF CELEBRITY to Attract New Customers and Obliterate Your Competition!

Charles W. Price, Esq.

COPYRIGHT

LIABILITY DISCLAIMER

CONTACT INFO

Up Your ACE Marketing, LLC
400 Maitland Avenue
Altamonte Springs, FL 32701
1-833-IM-AN-ACE (1-833-462-6223)

www.UpYourACE.com

Got Questions? Need Help?

In this book, you'll find the secrets to success that I've discovered over the last 20+ years. I've learned most of those secrets the hard way - trial and error, lots of heartache, tens of thousands of hours, and hundreds of thousands of dollars.

I now dedicate my time and energy to helping other entrepreneurs, professionals and small business owners learn these secrets the easy way.

I created my coaching and training company, Up Your A.C.E.!, because I believe that all entrepreneurs, professionals and small business owners should become THE Authority, Celebrity and Expert in their niche. If you're ready to take the next step, and explode your income and your profit, I invite you to explore the many training and coaching programs that we offer.

For more information, go to www.UpYourACE.com, or call 1-833-IM AN ACE (833-462-6223).

Up Your A.C.E.!
Authority · Celebrity · Expertise

Acknowledgments

The author gratefully acknowledges the following people for their support and contributions:

My wife, Suzi, my biggest supporter, cheerleader and muse, who edited my manuscript and picked up the slack for our family while I created the video courses, prepared and gave presentations and wrote this book.

My family, who had to live without me for a while as I completed all of the above.

The many mentors who have shaped my understanding of marketing, including, in no particular order, Dan Kennedy, Dave Dee, Joel Bauer, Suzanne Evans, Larry Winget, Russell Brunson and Eric Lofholm. The list is really much longer than this!

My personal coaching students who have helped me to refine the way I teach the creation of Authority, Celebrity and Expertise and have put their trust in me.

The thousands of clients who have entrusted me with their financial lives throughout the years. I've learned as much from them as they've learned from me.

Introduction

Hello. My name is Charlie Price. I'm a Florida attorney and the author of six books, including the one that you're reading now. I wrote each and every one of those books because they helped to establish me as THE Authority, Celebrity and Expert in every niche that I wanted to dominate. As a result, I've gone from struggling attorney to thriving business owner in ever niche that I've targeted.

But, it took me a while to learn the secret to success. When I first opened my own law firm many years ago, I really struggled financially. In fact, I barely made enough money to pay the rent and put food on the table. Why? Because no one knew who I was and there were a lot of attorneys offering the same legal services.

To the average client or referral partner, I was just like any other attorney – a commodity. And, just like any commodity, they wanted the lowest price that they could find. If I didn't offer the lowest price, they would just go down the street to the next attorney who WAS willing to give them the lowest price. And, there were a lot of attorneys who were willing to do just that.

So, I played the game. I lowered my prices to compete with other attorneys – and I had to work twice as hard as a result. I took every client that came through the door – even though they weren't a good fit for me and they made my life miserable. I

1

took work that other attorneys didn't want – and gave those attorneys a huge cut of the fees for my trouble.

Does any of this sound familiar? Are you struggling financially because you're competing on price with your competition? Are you cutting your fees and working more than you should? If your prospects and referral sources think of you as a commodity, then you're going to be competing on price – and you're going to be miserable. Believe me, I understand.

But, the secret is to NOT compete as a commodity. You need to stop playing by the rules that you know and change the game. You need to learn the secret to setting yourself apart from the competition.

Over the years, I've learned that the REAL secret to setting yourself apart from all of your competition is the perception that your clients, customers, prospects and referral partners have about you, your service and your products. That's right. I said the PERCEPTION that your clients, prospects and referral partners have about you!

You see, I've discovered a simple secret that has transformed me from struggling attorney to thriving business owner. And I'm going to share that secret with you in this book.

This simple secret has literally changed my life. And what is that secret?

BECOME A CELEBRITY IN YOUR NICHE!

Throughout this book, we'll explore this secret in more detail and I'll show you exactly how you can use it to go from commodity to celebrity in less than 30 days.

There are many ways to use the secret of celebrity, and I'll touch on several of them in this book. However, I believe that the FIRST step to establishing yourself as a celebrity in your niche is to write a book – to become a published author. I believe this is true for most professionals, business owners, entrepreneurs, executives, and anyone else who wants to set themselves apart from the competition.

As a published author, people PERCEIVE that you are an expert, celebrity and authority in the topic of your book. Now, hopefully you really are an expert in the topic area of your book. But, you really just need to know more than your reader does about that topic.

I've written books about bankruptcy, foreclosure defense and tax resolution. And, although I almost certainly know more about those topics than most of my readers, I know that there are other attorneys that know more about these topics than me – even in my local area.

But, it doesn't matter. All that matters is that potential clients and referral partners know that I wrote the book on a certain topic and PERCEIVE that I am THE Authority, Celebrity and Expert in that area. As a result, they chase me to represent them or to refer clients to me.

As an Authority, Celebrity and Expert in my niches – because I wrote the book on it – I can charge a premium for my services because clients want me to represent them at any cost. I'm no longer competing with every other attorney who offers the same services that I offer, even when they offer the exact same services. Because, I'm the Authority, Celebrity and Expert in that area and those other attorneys are not.

My guess is that you believe me on some level and would love to write your own book. But, I can almost hear the doubt creeping into your mind right now. I think I know what you're thinking.

If you're like most of the people that I've worked with over the years to write their own books, you're probably first thinking that you don't have the time to write a book – right? I hear this almost every time that I suggest that someone write a book.

"I'm working 60+ hours a week running my business. I don't have time to write a book. I barely have time to see my family and friends. How can I set aside the time to write a book?"

Is that running through your mind? Forget it! In this book, I'm going to show you how to write and publish your own book in 30 days or less – working just one hour a day. For now, you're just going to have to trust me and keep reading. Using the techniques that I'm going to show you, I wrote and published my last book in 9 days! You can do that, too!

The second major reason that I hear from most of my students as to why they can't write a book is because they're not "good" writers. So, I'm also going to show you why this is also just a myth. You do NOT need to be a "good" writer to write a great book. You just need to be able to communicate. And, we're all able to communicate in some way.

I'm going to show you how to write a great book – FAST – even if you can't write and hate to write. In fact, you won't need to write anything. Sound good? Again, just trust me and keep reading.

So, by writing you own book, you will become the instant Authority and Expert in that topic because you wrote the book. Then, you'll need to become a Celebrity. You do that by promoting your book and yourself to your potential prospects and referral partners. I'm going to show you how to do that as well.

By the time you finish this book, you'll know exactly how to write and publish your own book, and how to use that book to become the Celebrity in you niche. As a result, potential clients, customers, and referral partners will chase you for your services and products. You'll be able to charge a premium for your services or products, and you'll make more money and work less than you do now.

This book is for all the entrepreneurs, professionals, coaches, speakers and small business owners who want to learn how to use the Secret of

Celebrity to Attract New Customers and Obliterate Their Competition. It's for everyone who has the perfect service or product to solve their customer's challenges, but can't get those customers to notice them. It's for everyone that wants to stop competing on price and start exploding their income. And, it's for you, if you're ready!

So, if you're ready to change your life, let's go!

Section 1 – The Secret of Celebrity

In this section, we're going to dig deep into the Secret of Celebrity. I'm going to share my tale of woe, and tell you how I transformed my law firm with the Secret. Then, I'll reveal the Four Secrets to put you on your path to becoming THE Authority, Celebrity and Expert in your niche!

CHAPTER 1: ARE YOU A CELEBRITY OR A COMMODITY?

I was in Las Vegas not long ago. I was just minding my own business, and walking through one of the cavernous indoor malls associated with a high-end casino.

All of a sudden, I was pushed aside - now, I mean physically pushed aside – by this huge, muscular guy who was as wide as he was tall. I noticed, as he pushed on my chest, that he had an earpiece and that he was part of a group of men who were pushing everyone out of the way.

I started to think that maybe my huge friend was a Secret Service agent and that his security detail was clearing the path for the President of the United States. So, like the rest of the crowd, I stood back and watched for the President and his entourage to make his way through the crowd.

But, instead of the President, I saw the familiar backside of …. Kim Kardashian! That's right! I was pushed aside by Kim Kardashian's security detail!

At first, I was pretty upset. I didn't like that someone had physically pushed me aside. I didn't like it even more because I was pushed aside for Kim Kardashian.

Now look, I don't have anything against Kim Kardashian. But, she's not the President of the United States. Why should I get pushed aside for Kim Kardashian just because she's a "celebrity"?

But then, when I calmed down a bit, I started to think that my experience was really a great example of what happens to most of us in the real world. If you're just an average person walking through life, the chances are that you're going to get pushed aside – or overlooked – by the crowd in favor of the celebrities. People will step aside to watch as the celebrities make their way through the crowd – and everyone else is just the crowd.

So, let me ask you a question, and I want you to answer honestly. Are you getting pushed aside by the Kim Kardashians of your industry? People who may not even have your abilities or products, but who have the celebrity status that you lack?

Are your potential prospects, clients, customers and referral sources watching the celebrities in your industry and ignoring you because you're just part of the crowd? Are you trying to make your way to the front of the crowd to get noticed, but keep getting pushed back because you're not a celebrity?

If you want to stand out from the crowd and get noticed, YOU need to become a Celebrity. Now look, I'm not necessarily talking about becoming the star of your own reality television show. But, there are MANY ways to become a Celebrity.

Unfortunately, most require a lot of luck – and sometimes a lot of money.

Fortunately, for most of us, you don't need to become a celebrity on a national level. Instead, you should focus on becoming a big fish in a little pond. You need to stand out from the crowd in your niche or geographical area so that potential customers and referral sources will stop what they're doing and watch you. I've found that this is the quickest way to dramatically increase your income and become the master of your own business or practice.

I Struggled to Learn the Secret

Unfortunately, I learned this lesson the hard way. I experienced a lot of heartache and near financial collapse before I finally learned the secrets that I'm going to share with you in this book. So, I want to show you the easy way to get what you want in your business. And, that starts with showing you what NOT to do – because I've already done it!

When I first graduated from law school, many years ago, I got a job at a big law firm. It was really a dream job for a young lawyer. And, at that time, I thought my path to success was a straight path. I'd work for a few years, become a partner in the law firm, and retire on easy street. But, I quickly learned that life – and the path to success – is rarely a straight line.

You know how it goes. You start out with one path in mind, but life takes you on a completely different path. So, after many years of working at big law firms, including a three-year side career teaching legal writing at the Florida State University College of Law, I decided it was time for a change.

My wife had just given birth to our second child and I wanted to stop working 80 hours a week to spend more time with my family. So, I decided that it would be a great idea to open my own law firm.

Why not, right? I'm a pretty smart guy and a decent attorney. I thought it would be easy! I'd be able to make more money and spend more time with my family. What could go wrong?

So, not only did I quit my high-paying law firm job, I also convinced my wife - who was also an attorney – to quit her law firm job, too!

So, we started our own law firm with high hopes. And guess what?

We nearly died that first year in business! I was miserable and overworked, and hardly made any money.

We struggled because no one knew who I was. To my potential clients, I was just another attorney. They didn't care that I did well in law school or had worked at big law firms. They didn't care that I had been a professor.

No, I was just another attorney like all the other attorneys - and attorneys were a dime a dozen. Clients just wanted the cheapest price for the service.

To them, I was just a commodity. I was just as good, or bad, as every other attorney. So, I STILL had to work 80 hours a week because I wasn't charging enough for my services – and I was only making a fraction of what I earned at the big law firms. Until, I finally learned the secret ...

To survive, we rented office space from another attorney in town and handled cases for him that he didn't want. He didn't want those cases because they were miserable cases with miserable clients. But, it was money. That attorney took 50% of the fees, and I did all the work. I was grateful for the money – but miserable. Until I learned the secret ...

How I Learned the Secret

The secret that changed my life really came from desperation. We all have those times in our lives where we can vividly remember EXACTLY what happened at some particular moment. Usually these memories are some of our best - or worst - moments in our life. One of those for me – and I can still FEEL it like it was yesterday - was when I figured out how to escape from my trap.

I was up late. It was about 11:30pm. My wife and children were long asleep. But, I was wide awake in the living room trying to figure out what I was going to do. We weren't making enough money to pay the bills.

I didn't know if I was going to be able to pay our mortgage or office rent. I also didn't know if I was going to be able to pay our one employee – a secretary that my wife had brought with her from her law firm. I was thinking that I was going to have to go back to the big law firms – and that made me want to throw up.

I was literally sick to my stomach with worry. But, I knew that I had to do something. So, I had heard somewhere that you should write direct mail letters to clients and that you should write a book.

So, that night, I cranked out a direct mail letter to people who were facing lawsuits. At the end of the letter, in a P.S., I mentioned that I had written a book called *Life After Bankruptcy*. And, that's when EVERYTHING changed!

Literally a day after I mailed that letter, I started getting calls from people desperately wanting to speak with me about their financial problems. When they came for their appointments, they all said the same thing – "Are you the guy that wrote that book?"

I know that they hadn't read the book, because I got most of these people in the door immediately. But, it didn't matter. They wanted to hire me because I wrote the book on surviving life after bankruptcy.

They knew that they needed to file bankruptcy, and they wanted to hire THE Authority, Celebrity and Expert in bankruptcy. And, apparently that was me because I wrote *Life After Bankruptcy*. I was shocked – but thrilled!

Potential clients stepped aside to watch me and ignored the other attorneys in the crowd. I became the Celebrity in my niche in Orlando, and I started to enjoy celebrity income as a result.

My schedule went from wide open to completely booked in one week. I went from financial death to financial prosperity, literally overnight. I started getting so many new clients that I had to hire more and more staff to handle all the new cases. Finally, I outgrew the office that we shared with other attorneys and moved into our own location.

In less than two years, I became the number one filer of bankruptcy cases in Orlando. All because I wrote a book and became the Celebrity in bankruptcy in my area!

So, do you know what I learned the hard way? Being a good lawyer and making money are two entirely different things. At the big law firms, I was used to getting a big fat paycheck every other week and all I had to do was be a good lawyer and work 80 hours a week.

But, when you're in business for yourself, it's NOT enough to be good at what you do and to work a lot. Some of the best lawyers I know – and other professionals and business owners – are starving and getting ready to close their doors because they can't get customers in the door or make enough money from the clients that they have.

Are you struggling right now in your business? Maybe you're not ready to close the doors, but maybe you're really not where you want to be financially?

If you're like I was, I think the struggle comes from having too many other professionals and business owners competing for the same business. I struggled that first year on my own because there were too many other lawyers competing for business. Law schools keep cranking out more and more attorneys and those new attorneys will work for nothing to get any money coming in the door. And, I also competed with attorneys and law firms who were pouring massive amounts of money into advertising.

And, no one knew who I was. To potential clients and referral sources, I was just another attorney – no better or worse – than any other attorney. I wasn't special – I was just another attorney – a commodity.

Are you a commodity? Do enough people know who you are? Are you different from everyone else? Or, are you fighting with everyone for the same customers and dollars? When I first opened my own law firm, I was struggling with all of those things. And, I was miserable – and broke!

It was only when I became a Celebrity – by writing my own book – that people started to notice me. The crowd of other attorneys were just commodities to potential clients and referral sources. I had stepped away from the crowd of those other attorneys and was walking down the red carpet – simply because I wrote a book.

The Big Secret – You Make More Income for WHO You Are, Rather Than WHAT You Do!

This may not be the secret that you thought I was going to tell you. But, it's really the key to everything that I AM going to tell you.

I learned this secret from one of my mentors – Dan Kennedy. (I also used one of Dan's courses to write that first direct mail sales letter.)

So, here's the secret to unlocking your financial prosperity – You make more money for WHO you are, rather than WHAT you do.

I think that's worth repeating! YOU MAKE MORE MONEY FOR WHO YOU ARE, RATHER THAN WHAT YOU DO!

To illustrate this point, let me ask you a question. Who makes more money? A teacher? Or a celebrity?

In 2016, the average elementary school teacher earned $43,557.00. Kim Kardashian earned $51 million. I think that you'll agree that the difference in income has very little to do with ability and everything to do with celebrity.

Now, I don't make $51 million per year. But, I do earn a substantially higher income than most of my competitors. And, it's all because I learned this basic secret about WHO you are rather than WHAT you do!

There are a LOT of attorneys that offer bankruptcy services. In the consumers' eyes, most of these attorneys are just a commodity – and they want to hire the cheapest commodity that they can find.

But, my book elevated me out of the mass of commodity attorneys and into a different level – a level where the clients chased me to represent them – and not me chasing them. The Authority, Celebrity and Expertise of the book put me into a different category from every other attorney that I was competing against.

As I expanded my law firm to handle other practice areas, I wrote separate books to promote those different practice areas and establish me as the Authority, Celebrity and Expert in those areas as well. In every one of those practice areas, I became one of the top providers of those services in Orlando.

But, truthfully, I am NOT the best attorney in those areas - there are many attorneys that I think are much better than me. But, it doesn't matter because people WANT ME - because I wrote the book. They want me because of WHO I am, rather than WHAT I do. I WANT THAT FOR YOU TOO!!

Ultimately, there are many ways to establish you as the Celebrity in your niche. But, I believe it all starts with being the author of your own book. So, I'm going to show you exactly how to become a published author, and how to do it fast.

To help you on your journey, I'm going to share with you my four secrets to writing a great book fast. And, the secrets may surprise you!

So, let's look at those four secrets now.

CHAPTER 2: THE FOUR SECRETS TO WRITING A GREAT BOOK - FAST

I've told you that the secret to my success was that I learned to stand apart from the crowd of other professionals by writing my own book. I've done this over and over. The formula is very simple.

First, I decide what niche I want to dominate. Next, I write a book that targets that niche. That makes me an instant Authority and Expert in that niche. Then, I promote the book to prospects and referral sources. That makes me the Celebrity in the niche. Finally, I watch the money roll in as clients chase me to represent them.

It's really just that simple. And, I'm not the only one who has found great success in their business by writing books. In a recent survey, 96% of all professionals who had written a book reported that they had seen a significant increase in their business and income as a direct result of writing a book.

But, in another survey, although 81% of all professionals agreed that they SHOULD write a book, only 1% of them actually did write a book. 1%!!

Why is that? If my secret to success is so simple, why don't more people write books to become celebrities in their niches and dramatically increase their income?

I think the real problem comes down to mindset and technique. But, if you can conquer the mindset issues that stop the average person dead in their tracks, and then learn the techniques, you WILL write a great book – FAST!

To make this easy, I've distilled the process down to four secrets. Once you learn the four secrets, and IMPLEMENT them, you WILL be able to write and publish your own book.

In this chapter, we'll discuss those secrets - #1 – Your Big Why; #2 – Overcoming the Mental Obstacles; #3 – Time Blocking and a Writing Plan; and #4 – The Techniques.

So, let's look at those secrets now.

Secret #1 - Your Big Why

I think the biggest secret to actually writing and publishing a book is your big WHY! If you can FEEL the reason for writing a book deep down in your bones, you'll actually get it done – and in record time!

Now, I know what you're thinking. This sounds like new-age garbage. I get it. But, think back through your life. Think about some of your major accomplishments. How did you get through the challenges and actually complete your goal?

My guess is that your BIG WHY was so strong that nothing could stop you. If you really want to write a book, that's the energy that you need to tap.

Look. I know that the thought of writing a book is daunting. But, if you really want it bad enough, you'll breeze right through it. We just need to find your right reasons – your big WHY or Whys.

One of my early mentors was Todd Duncan. I owned two mortgage-related businesses at one time, and Todd Duncan was one of the gurus of the mortgage industry, and an incredibly gifted motivational speaker. In his book, *The Power to Be Your Best,* Todd talks about getting to your REAL Why.

For most of us, me included, if you ask us why we want to have more customers, or sell more products or services, it's to make money. If I ask you why you want to write a book, you'll probably say that you want to make more money. Right?

But, for most people, just making more money isn't enough motivation to actually propel you through something that seems really hard – like writing a book. So, I want to spend a few minutes talking about Todd Duncan's strategy for getting to the REAL WHY. And, it's actually pretty easy.

First, ask this question. What's important to you about writing a book? You'll probably say that you want to make more money.

But, the next question is – What's important to you about wanting to make more money? For me, the answer is that I need to take care of my family.

But, the next question is – What's important to you about taking care of your family? Now, I have to tell you that the answer to this question really depends on where you are in your life. I've had two answers to this question, at different stages of my life.

There have been many times when the answer was simply that I needed to make sure that my family had food to eat, that the electricity and water worked, and that we all had a place to live. There's been more than once where desperation was my motivator. I've got six children, and it costs a lot of money to keep a family of eight going.

So, I've done some of my best, and quickest, writing when desperation was the sole motivator. And, it's a strong motivator. If you ask me if there's anything more important than taking care of my family, I'll tell you no. That's how you know that you've finally reached your true core motivator.

However, once you actually have enough money to satisfy your core motivator, it won't motivate you anymore. I've had several times in my career where my income continued to increase, then leveled off. I couldn't increase it from there.

Ultimately, I figured out that the reasons for the plateau in income really had to do with a lack of clarity about my motivation – my Big WHY. You see, once I met my family's basic needs, I didn't have anything else pushing me forward. I've had to go back through the exercise several times over the years to reevaluate what my core motivator was.

This will probably be true for you as well. For now, however, just focus on where you are now and what your core motivation is. You'll know that you've hit you're your core motivator once you can say "No" to the question "Is there anything more important about that to you?"

So now that my family's basic needs are provided for, the next question is – What's important to you about taking care of your family? For me, the answer now is that I want to make sure that I have enough free time – and money - to have grand experiences with my family.

But, the next question is "What's important to you about having enough free time – and money – to have grand experiences with my family?" For me, the answer is that I want to live life, and experience life, and learn everything that I can about the world as I go. And, I want to share all of those experiences with my family.

If you ask me if there's anything more important than that to me, I'll tell you no. If I need to get excited and motivated to complete a project – like writing a book – all that I need to do is picture going on an extended vacation around the world with my family. That will get me going every time.

Expensive cars and big houses don't motivate me. But, I know many other people have their own deeply motivating reasons for wanting expensive cars and big houses. That's great. The point is that you MUST find the thing – or things – that motivate you at your core.

You may really be surprised by the results of this exercise. When I first did it, I nearly cried. It was as if the blindfold had finally been pulled from my eyes and I could see for the first time. It's truly transformational.

If you can tap into that true core motivator at the center of your soul, you'll be able to power through writing your first book, and your second and third, and not be deterred by the roadblocks and obstacles that will inevitably appear to stop you.

So, do yourself a favor. ACTUALLY DO THIS EXERCISE! I promise that this will help you write and finish your book!

Now, AFTER you've discovered your core motivator (And, I really mean after you've done the exercise!), I want to talk about the second part of the mindset that you need to get your book done – overcoming the myths and mental blocks.

The first part of this chapter has been about discovering the motivation to blow through the obstacles. The next part is going to be about shining the light of truth on the myths and mental blocks that you're going to tell yourself are real reasons for not starting or finishing your book.

But, I'm going to show you that these myths and mental blocks are just lies. Once you realize that, nothing will stop you!

Secret #2 - Overcoming the Myths and Mental Blocks

Although most people KNOW that they should write a book to promote themselves and their services, almost everyone has several preconceived opinions about writing a book that stops them in their tracks.

But, these preconceived opinions are really just myths. And, these myths keep most people out of the 1% Club and stuck in the commodity trap.

So, let's talk about those myths now. I'm going to show you that they really are just myths. And, if you can get past the head-games, you can make a LOT of money by writing your own book – even if you don't think that you really CAN write your own book!

Myth #1 – I Don't Have Time to Write a Book/It Takes Too Long to Write a Book

The number one myth that I hear from people as to why they've never written a book is that they don't have time to write a book and that it takes too long to write a book. I hear it all the time. People say "I'm working full-time and I've got commitments to my friends and family. I don't have any time left to do anything. I certainly don't have time to write a book!"

I used to think that it takes a long time to write a book, too. I mentioned earlier that I accepted a teaching position at the Florida State University College of Law after law school. What I didn't tell you was that I took that job primarily to write my first book – *Life After Bankruptcy.*

I took a 50% cut in pay to teach at Florida State. But, I knew that I would have a lot of free time to work on that first book.

And, I really did have a lot of free time to work on that book. That was good, because it took me NINE MONTHS to write *Life After Bankruptcy*, working virtually full-time.

So now you're probably thinking that I really am crazy. Most people don't have the ability to change jobs and work full-time on a book. I just proved the point that most people really don't have the time to write a book.

But, the truth is writing a book does NOT need to take nine months. In fact, I wrote my last book in NINE DAYS while working full-time in my law firm and tax resolution company. The secret to writing fast is the system, and I'm going to share that system with you in this book.

Unfortunately, I didn't have that system when I wrote *Life After Bankruptcy.* It took me many years, and a lot of trial and error, to create the exact system to write a great book fast. Fortunately, you get the benefit of all my years of trial and error.

So, how long SHOULD it take to write your book. To write my last book in 9 days, I worked Saturday and Sunday, one hour a day the following week, and the following Saturday and Sunday.

If you want a more relaxed pace, I think that you can write and publish your own book in 30 days, if you plan ahead and take bite-sized pieces. I'm talking about from start to finish – from blank page to published book – with all of the pieces that make a book look and feel like a book that was published by a traditional publishing house.

And, to show you that you really DO have the time to write your own book, I'm going to show you how you can actually write your own book in one afternoon – if you know the secret!

I'm going to show you the secret to writing a great book fast in the coming pages. For now, I want you to set aside your belief that it takes too long to write a book and that you don't have the time. I'm just asking you to trust me for a little while.

I've helped countless students to write their books fast. So, I know that it's possible. You CAN do it! You just have to believe that you CAN do it!

Myth #2 – I Can't Write a Book Because I'm not a "Good" Writer/I Hate to Write!

The second myth that prevents people from joining the 1% Club is that many people think that they're not "good" writers or that they really hate to write. The thought of sitting down and typing out a book is right up there with giving a public speech in the nude!

But, this is really also just a myth. You DON'T need to be a good writer – you just need to communicate. And, we can all communicate.

You don't actually need to be what we consider to be a "good" writer. You just need to talk and be yourself. Writing like you talk is a lot better than being a "good" writer or even a great writer.

Let me tell you an embarrassing personal story to illustrate this point. As a lawyer, I was considered to be an excellent writer. In fact, I had received several awards in law school and subsequently taught legal writing at the Florida State University College of Law – because I was a "good" writer.

So, when I wrote my first book, I sent the manuscript to several people for their opinion – fully expecting them to ooh and ah over my excellent writing skills.

Unfortunately, I received the same response from nearly everyone that read it – the book SOUNDED like it was written by a lawyer – and it was boring. Most of them couldn't even make it through the whole manuscript!

At first, I was slightly offended. But, then I put my ego aside and realized that the book wasn't about me – it was about the reader. If the reader can't understand – or doesn't want to understand – the material, then you're just wasting your time as a writer.

So, instead of writing like a lawyer, I decided to write like I talk. I used conversational language and tried to make the text as simple to understand as possible. In fact, at that time there was a software program that would analyze your text and assign a school-level equivalent to the text. My goal was to get the readability level down to a 6th grade level.

Ultimately, I accomplished that goal. I revised the entire manuscript and again sent it out for reviews. This time, the reviews were much more favorable. People actually understood what I was saying and were actually interested.

Ever since then, I've tried to write like a speak – even when I'm drafting complex legal briefs or memorandums. EVERYONE appreciates a simple writing style – even judges.

My point in telling you this story is for you to get over the idea that you need to be a great writer to write a book. Really, you just need to be able to talk about the topic that you're going to write about. If you can talk about the topic with friends, family, or potential customers – you're going to produce a great book.

Can you talk to your customers about your topic? Yes, you can. You do it all the time. If you can do that, you CAN write a book!

Several of my favorite techniques for quickly writing a book involve NO actual writing at all – just talking. And, I'm going to share those techniques with you in a later chapter. So, I don't want you to get caught up in the idea that you'll never write a book because of your writing ability – or lack thereof – because it's simply not true!

Myth #3 – I Can't Write a Book Because I'm Not an Authority or Expert

Although I hear this myth less often that the first two, this particular myth keeps a lot of people from entering the 1% Club. Most people think that you must first be considered an authority or expert by your niche BEFORE you can write a book. But, for most people, I think this is backwards.

I do believe that you must know more about your topic than your reader. For most of my readers, this is certainly true. The point of writing a book is to promote your services or products to a niche market that you serve or want to serve. That generally means that you have a certain level of ability or product capability in that niche.

So, this myth really goes to something more. It goes to a writer's fear of inadequacy and that competitors in their niche may judge them because these competitors haven't anointed the potential writer as the "authority" or "expert" in that niche.

So, what is an "authority" or "expert"? Who gets to decide if you're an authority or expert or not? Do you think that I asked other bankruptcy attorneys if they thought I was an authority or expert and worthy of writing my first book? What do you think they would have said?

You know what I say? Who cares? I'm an authority and expert BECAUSE I wrote the book. YOU will also be an authority and expert BECAUSE you write your book. That's the secret.

So, don't worry if you think that your competition doesn't consider you to be an authority or expert. First, it's probably not true. Second, even if it is true, you'll get the last laugh.

Don't worry what your competition thinks about you. Worry instead about what your potential customers think about you. And, your potential customers will think that you're an authority and expert when you write your own book!

Myth #4 – I'm Not Certified or Don't Have a Degree

This myth is similar to the myth about being an "authority" or "expert" before you can write a book. A lot of people tell me that they can't write a book because they're not "certified" or don't have a degree in the topic of the book.

This myth also goes to a feeling of inadequacy. Somehow, we all feel worthy only if we are certified by some group or have a degree from some institution. Why is that?

What is different about you when you possess some certification or degree? Some of the most famous and successful people I know don't have a certification or degree in their area. And yet, no one cares.

For example, Tony Robbins is arguably one of the most successful and well-known motivational gurus in the world. And yet, he never went to college and doesn't have a certification in anything. He now offers certification programs, but he doesn't have one himself. This doesn't seem to matter to anyone who pays him lots of money to learn his secrets. It shouldn't matter to you either.

I could give you a list of hundreds of hugely successful authors that have no certification or degree, but didn't let that stop them. But, you really don't need a list. You only need to believe that you're offering something of value to your readers.

Let your readers decide if they think your lack of certification or degree is important to them. But, I can guarantee that they won't care if you improve their life in some way.

What matters is the value that you provide to your reader. Are you providing value to your reader? Then, you're all set.

Secret # 3 - Time Blocking and a Writing Plan

Along with learning the technique to discover my Big Why, I credit time blocking with having the most impact on my professional life. And, coincidently, I learned both techniques from Todd Duncan. I mentioned Todd Duncan in the earlier section.

Time blocking is really just a process of scheduling appointments with yourself to actually get things done. The point is to schedule the MOST important things in your calendar, before you schedule anything else. That way, the really important things get done first.

Unfortunately, most of us do just the opposite and fill our days with the unimportant activities. Why do we do that? Probably because they're easy. But, they distract us from doing the things that we really NEED to do to accomplish the goals that we KNOW that we want to achieve. We fill our day with these unimportant, time-wasting activities, and consume much of the day.

Then, when we've wasted enough time, we start to focus on more important activities. Although these aren't total time-wasters, they STILL don't propel us to our REAL GOALS – our BIG WHYS.

So, by the time we start to focus on our BIG WHYS – the REALLY important things that will REALLY propel us to our goals, there's NO TIME LEFT!

This is why people tell me that they don't have time to write a book. There's no time left at the end of the day – or week or month – because they've filled all of their time with activities that aren't really that important. They can't work on the most important tasks because they've filled their day with everything else.

So, if you want to actually get your book written and published, you MUST schedule the time in your schedule to WRITE the book. If you schedule your writing and publishing tasks into your schedule first, everything else that you're doing now will magically fit into your schedule.

I know what you're thinking – "I barely have time enough to handle my current tasks. If I start adding in extra time to write a book, things are going to slip, clients are going to be mad, the staff will run around without direction, the business will go up in flames." Yes, I've said all of those things too. But, you know what? These are just FEARS – False Expectations Appearing Real.

I've discovered over the years that everything still gets done, even when I schedule major activities into my schedule. If I'm away from the office for a day, or two, or three, to write a book or work on a marketing campaign, everyone survives. The clients still get serviced, the staff manages, and the business survives.

But, magically, you start to complete the really important tasks. Magically, you complete your first book, and then your second and your third.

So, how do you start time blocking to write your book? Let me show you the process.

The Process

I'm going to show you a process that you can use to plan and time block any goal. I learned this process from Dave Dee, a master of marketing, magic, influence and organization. The actual process is much longer than what I'm going to present. But, I'll give you exactly what you need to plan and time block your book.

Brain-Dump Your Tasks

The first step for time blocking and scheduling your writing plan is to identify as many tasks as possible for completing your goal. In this case, we want to identify all of the tasks needed to write and publish your book. I'm going to help you out and give you my list:

Identify Your Target Market
Pick a Topic
Choose a Framework
Create the Outline
Write Your Rough Draft
Create the Perfect Title and Subtitle
Write the Title Page
Write the Copyright and Legal Stuff Page
Create the Table of Contents
Write the Acknowledgments Page
Write the Introduction
Write the Conclusion
Edit the Book
Format and Typeset the Book
Create the Book Cover
Publish the Book

Identify How Long Each Task Will Take to Complete

The next step is to identify how long it will take you to complete each task. I know that you don't know this exactly. I tend to underestimate how long it will take me to do everything. You may find that you do this as well. That's OK. Just do your best to estimate, and you can adjust your schedule later as needed.

I'm going to give you suggested completion times for each task on the next page. But, remember that I tend to underestimate my goals and I've done this before. I've tried to account for this in the schedule. So, don't worry if it takes you longer to accomplish any or all of the tasks. All that matters is that you DO get everything done.

Task	Time to Complete
Identify Your Target Market	1 Hour
Pick a Topic For Your Book	1 Hour
Choose a Framework For Writing Your Book	1 Hour
Create the Outline, Including Chapters and Sub-Chapters	2 Hours
Write Your Rough Draft	15 Hours
Create the Perfect Title and Subtitle	1 Hours
Write the Title Page	½ Hour
Write the Copyright and Legal Stuff Page	½ Hour
Create the Table of Contents	2 Hours
Write the Acknowledgements Page	½ Hour
Write the Introduction	1 Hour
Write the Conclusion	1 Hour
Edit the Book (Using an Editor)	2 Hours
Format and Typeset the Book (With a Designer)	1 Hours
Create the Book Cover (With a Designer)	2 Hours
Publish the Book on CreateSpace	1 Hours
Totals	32 ½ Hours

Wow! That's what you're probably thinking. Right? How am I going to fit 32 ½ hours into my schedule? Well, let's think about that.

Let's say that you want to write and publish your book in 30 days – and you should! If you divide 32 ½ hours by 30 days, you need to work on your book 1.08 hours a day. That's not too bad. Where else can you work 1.08 hours a day to double or triple your income? And, you can divide this up in whatever way best suits your schedule.

So, for example, you can do what I did and write during the weekend. Let's say that you work just over 8 hours a day during each weekend. (For my last book, I worked 20 hours each weekend for two weekends.) That will give you the 32 ½ hours that you need to finish the book.

So, like me, you can have your ENTIRE book done, from blank page to published book, in 9 DAYS! You CAN do this!

When you chunk your tasks this way, you start to see the possibilities. You know the old saying, "What's the best way to eat an elephant?" The answer? "One bite at a time!"

So, the best way to actually write and publish your book in 30 days or less is one bite at a time. When you break the tasks down like this, and assign completion times, you can see the bite-sized pieces, and the end doesn't look quite as daunting as it might otherwise look.

Time Block the Tasks Into Your Schedule

Now that we've identified the pieces, it's time to actually put them into your schedule. This is where the real magic happens.

To do this, decide how long you're going to devote to writing and publishing your book and when. So, if you're going to write one hour a day and one day each weekend, block that time in your calendar. If you're going to work five hours one day a week, block that time in your calendar. It's up to you.

But, you MUST actually block the time in your calendar and commit to using that time to write and publish your book. Remember, you must put the major tasks first!

Normally, I'm away from the office at least one day a week to work on some major task – like writing a book. I have scheduled as little as one hour in the calendar, to as many as three days a week. It usually depends on what I have going on at that moment and what I'm trying to accomplish.

I would suggest that you commit to working on your book AT LEAST one hour a day – more would be better. If you want to get your book done fast – and you should – devote more of your time to completing it.

Another thought about time blocking. When you block off time to work on your book – actually work on your book. Don't use the time to work on other seemingly pressing things. Don't check your email or Facebook or send text messages. Be present. Think about your big WHY. Picture what your life will be like when you have a completed book. This will help you to stay focused.

Right now, go to your calendar – I use Google Calendar – and block off the time to write your book. Make that time sacred and focus on writing. Before you know it, you'll have your published book in hand.

(For students of my premium online book publishing program, *Publishing Hacks*, I created a powerful demonstration on time blocking that I learned from Todd Duncan. It's been so popular with all of my students – as it was with me when I first saw it – that I've decided to offer it free to the readers of this book. So, if you go to www.UpYourACE.com/resources, you'll be able to watch the demonstration. It's very powerful. After seeing it, you may never work the same way again!)

Secret #4 – The Techniques

So, the final secret to writing a great book – fast – is to learn the techniques. I believe that many people stop writing their first book because they're using antiquated techniques that make writing and publishing a book take forever. So, in the next several chapters, I'm going to show you my secret hacks and techniques to get your book done in 30 days or less.

But first, we need to talk about the first things to consider, even before you start writing. Let's do that now.

Section 2 – Things to Consider Before You Start

I believe that most people never join the 1% Club in part because they don't properly plan the steps before they start writing. As a result, they quickly stall and give up.

I'm not going to let that happen to you! You can write a good book – FAST – if you think through and plan the initial steps before you ever start writing.

In this section, we're going to do just that!

First, in Chapter 3, we'll discuss the type of book you need to write and how to get it published.

Then, in Chapter 4, we'll get laser-focused on who you need to target with your book – your Ideal Customer.

Finally, in Chapter 5, we'll use your Ideal Customer profile to pick the perfect topic for your book – and make your Ideal Customer beg you for help!

If you're ready, let's go!

CHAPTER 3: WHAT KIND OF BOOK ARE YOU GOING TO WRITE AND WHO WILL PUBLISH IT?

Before you even start to write your book, there are several things that you should consider, including whether your book should be a physical book or eBook and who will publish it. You're probably thinking that I'm putting the cart before the horse, right? You haven't even started writing and I'm talking about how it's going to get published!

But, there's a method to my madness. I want you to be clear about our goal. To access the power of celebrity with your book, you need a REAL book that you can hand to clients, prospects, referral sources and media outlets. Although it's important to have a PDF version of your book to use for marketing (we'll talk about that later), you need a real, physical copy of your book to become a celebrity.

There are many courses and books that will teach you how to write small eBooks for sale on Amazon. Although you CAN make some money from doing this, the REAL money comes from establishing your Authority, Celebrity and Expertise with your book – and using that to sell your services and products.

I've made millions of dollars for my law firm and tax resolution company over the years simply by using my books to become a celebrity in my niches. You'd have to sell a LOT of eBooks to make that that kind of money. Most authors never make that kind of money from selling their books. But, that's the power of Celebrity!

So, I'm going to answer the first question for you. You need to write and publish a physical book. You can, and should, sell your book on Amazon and other outlets. But, the goal is to become a Celebrity in your niche, NOT to sell books! I'm going to show you exactly how to do this.

Who Will Publish the Book?

The next question is who will publish the book? Over the years, I've bought and studied nearly every book and course available on how to write and publish a book. Most of these courses teach people to write a manuscript, hire a literary agent, and hope that a publisher accepts your manuscript for publication. But, for most professionals and small business owners, this is not a good approach.

First, you need to find an agent who is willing to take a chance on you and promote your book to the traditional publishers. But, agents reject 96% of all submissions they receive. Those aren't great odds.

Next, you need to get a traditional publisher to accept your book. And, they accept an even smaller percentage. So, the chances of actually getting your book published by a traditional publisher are very small – even if you wanted to do this.

And, if a traditional publisher DID agree to publish your book, it will take a year or longer to actually get it to market. That's a lot more time wasted.

Finally, even if the agent agrees to represent your book, and the publisher agrees to publish it, and you're willing to wait a year to get it published, you'll only earn $1 to $2 per book for your efforts. The average royalty for a paperback book is 8% of the retail price.

So, if you sell a book for $19.95, you as the author will receive $1.60 for each book sold. Therefore, unless you sell a LOT of books, you're never going to make REAL money from the sale of the books.

Instead, I believe that most professionals and small business owners should self-publish their books. The world of self-publishing has changed dramatically since I wrote my first book.

As a result, it's never been easier to produce a book that looks exactly like any book sitting on a bookstore shelf. And, it can be very inexpensive to do this.

When I published my first book, I had to print 5,000 copies of my book to get an acceptable printing cost. Then, I had to store them. Initially, I had them stored all around my house. You have no idea how much space 5,000 copies of a book takes up until they're actually in your house.

Later, I got smarter and had the books delivered to a fulfillment warehouse. The warehouse would store the books and mail them to customers when they bought. But, buying in bulk was really the only way to print books at that time.

Fortunately, we live in a world where you can get your books published one at a time. It's called Print on Demand – or POD. Now, you can upload your finished book and covers to a company and have them print and fulfill the book orders as they come in. I normally order 100 or 200 at a time to hand to clients, prospects and potential referral sources.

There are a variety of companies that offer Print on Demand services. I'll tell you more about this in later chapters.

When you know the secrets, techniques and hacks, you can produce a great book, and do it fast. By the time you finish this book, you'll have the tools you need to publish your own book and you'll be on your way to becoming THE Celebrity, Authority, and Expert in your niche!

Aren't People Who Self-Publish Losers?

I know that there are people who will say that self-publishing is just for people who can't get a traditional publisher to accept their book. For many people, that may be true. I told you the odds of getting a traditional publisher to accept your book – and they're not great.

But, you shouldn't let that prevent you from being a published author. I've NEVER had a client, prospect, referral source or media outlet ask me about the publisher of my books. It simply doesn't matter to them.

And, you CAN get your book into book stores and libraries even if you self-publish – if that's what you want. I was able to get a wholesaler to promote my first book to bookstores and libraries across the country. And, I sold a lot of books – enough to pay off a mortgage.

But, I've made many multiples of that income from using my books to become the Celebrity in my niches by distributing FREE copies of my book. So, don't get distracted by the desire to sell your books in bookstores and to libraries.

Should You Ever Consider a Traditional Publisher?

Although I think that most professionals and small business owners should only consider self-publishing, I do believe that there may be some people who would benefit from having a traditional publisher produce their book. Generally, I think that this would only include people who are looking for a national audience, or people who are targeting large corporate clients.

But, even then, I believe that this is a very small subset of most professionals and small business owners. You can generally generate the same Celebrity status by self-publishing your own book and then promoting it well.

Vanity Publishing vs. Do-it-Yourself

Another option that you may consider to become a published author is to hire a company to handle most, or all, of the writing and publishing tasks. These companies are called vanity publishing houses.

They won't reject your book proposal because you're paying them to create and publish the book for you. They have nothing to lose because you front all of the costs associated with publishing the book.

Their services and fees range wildly. I've seen fees on the low end of $5,000.00 to well over $35,000.00 on the higher end. Most are honest and straightforward about what they can and will do for you. But, there have been problems in the industry in the past with unbroken promises and hidden fees.

So, just be careful if you decide to hire a vanity publishing company to help you publish your book. Make sure you understand – and get in writing – what they will and won't do for you and what everything will cost.

This may be a good option for the professional or small business owner who has more money than time. But, as we'll discuss in the next chapter, I believe that you should write multiple books to target different niches or sub-niches in your industry.

If you learn the secrets to write and publish a good book – fast – you won't need to pay $5,000.00 to $35,000.00 every time you want to write another book. And, instead of waiting six months or a year to get your book published by a vanity publisher, you can do it yourself and have a book in 30 days.

I want you to become the Celebrity in your niche in 30 days and not wait six months or a year for a vanity publisher to complete your book! So, I believe that most professionals and small business owners should self-publish their own books.

So, I'm going to show you exactly how to write a REAL book that you can use to promote yourself as the Authority, Celebrity and Expert in your niche in 30 days or less and NOT spend a fortune doing it. And, you can MAKE a fortune doing it!

(In addition to my premium self-paced publishing program – *Publishing Hacks* – I also offer limited Done-With-You and Done-For-You services. For more information, go to www.UpYourACE.com.

CHAPTER 4: WHO IS YOUR READER? WHO IS YOUR IDEAL CUSTOMER?

I believe that many authors don't give a lot of thought to WHO they're actually writing their book for. (I know that "whom" is grammatically correct.) Sure, they have a general sense that they're writing for someone who is interested in the topic. But, they don't truly picture that reader in their mind when they're creating the book.

Remember, we're writing and publishing a book to attract your customers and clients to you. Yes, I want you to become a celebrity. But, I want you to become a celebrity to the customers and clients that you want to work with.

So, before you choose the topic for your book and begin writing, it REALLY helps to have a clear idea of WHO you're actually trying to target with your book – and what they want and need. This is the target market for your book.

In this chapter, I'm going to help you identify your target market by identifying your ideal client, customer or prospect. To make this less tedious going forward, I'm going to refer to this person as your "Ideal Customer."

I know that you may already have your Ideal Customer in mind, and have a sense of what they want or need. However, I've found that it helps to get laser-focused on this.

This is an exercise that you should do with all of your marketing efforts. And remember, writing and publishing your book IS a form of marketing. Therefore, if you've already done this exercise and determined who your Ideal Customer is – and what they want and need - just use that information here to help you choose a topic for your book in the next chapter.

However, if you haven't ever really stopped to think about who your Ideal Customer is – or what they want and need - it's time to do it. So, in this chapter, we're going to spend some time trying to identify your Ideal Customer and their wants and needs. Then, we'll figure out what the topic of your book should be, based on this information.

Knowing WHO you're writing to, and WHAT transformation they're looking for, will help you to pick the ideal topic for your book. This information will also help you to determine the chapters of your book and how you write the book. But, more on that later.

In addition, once you KNOW who your Ideal Customer is, you'll be able to market your book, and your services and products, with laser-like precision. You'll know where your Ideal Customer spends their time, what motivates him/her, and how you can reach him/her. Knowing this information about your Ideal Customer is very powerful and will help you Up Your A.C.E.!

For now, let's find out who your Ideal Customer really is.

Your Ideal Customer Defined

To determine your Ideal Customer, think about your best current clients or customers. Who do you make the most money from? Who do you enjoy working with? If you could get rid of all your other clients or customers, who would you keep? Whoever remains may be your Ideal Customer.

When doing this, it helps to think about a particular client or customer and have them in mind while you do the worksheet. Once you have that Ideal Customer in mind, you need to think about all of the characteristics of that client or customer. We're going to talk about those characteristics in terms of demographics, psychographics and emotions.

Demographics are traits that you can quantify, like age, gender, marital status, etc. Psychographics are more subjective, and relate to the psychology or behavior of your ideal client or customer.

Emotional information includes the hopes, dreams, fears and pain of your ideal client or customer. Although much of the emotional information could be properly included in the psychographic profile, I like to break it out for purposes of writing a book. This will help you to really target the topic for your book and the chapters that you should include in your book.

I don't want you to get concerned that you just signed up for something that will get too technical and have your eyes glaze over. This will all make sense to you in a moment – I promise!

Demographic Information

First, let's think about whether your Ideal Customer belongs to a certain demographic group. As I said before, think of demographics as traits that you can quantify, including age, gender, and marital status. Why is this important?

Well, the topic of your book may be very different if you're writing it for a 70-year-old married man living on Social Security, versus a 19-year-old single woman who is still in college. It might also be different if you're writing it to a 56-year-old lawyer living in Chicago, versus a 35-year-old farmer living in rural Alabama. You get the idea.

So, think about that Ideal Customer of yours. Then, try to determine these demographic factors for that Ideal Customer:

Age
Gender
Marital Status
Children or Not
Occupation
Income
Geographic Location
Ethnic Background
Education
Home Ownership

Psychographic Information

Next, you need to think about the psychographic factors for your Ideal Customer. Psychographic factors examine your target's personality, and include the interests, activities and opinions of your Ideal Customer.

Demographic information is based on hard objective data and identifies WHO someone is. Psychographic information is based on subjective data and helps to identify someone's motivations. Another way to think about this is that psychographic factors are behavior-based, whereas demographic factors are data-based.

I don't want you to get distracted by this. There's a lot more to psychographic study than what I'm presenting here. I just want you to get a GENERAL sense of your ideal client. For now, just humor me.

So, think again about that ideal client or customer of yours. Then, try to determine these psychographic factors for that Ideal Customer:

Interests

What interests do they have? An interest is an area of curiosity or desire for knowledge. There are an infinite number of interests. These could include:

Family
Wealth
Physical Fitness

Health
Nutrition
Religion
Social

Activities

What activities do they participate in?
These are things that they DO. You might think of
activities as hobbies. These could include:

Reading
Golf
Bowling
Sewing
Fishing
Partying
Clubs/Groups
Volunteering

Opinions

What opinions do they have? About
politics? About religion? About anything? Ideally,
you'll want to focus on the opinions that relate
directly to your service or product. But, this isn't
essential.

Why is it important to understand the
psychographic data for your Ideal Customer?
Because it will help you to understand what makes
your Ideal Customer tick. What motivates them?
What makes them happy? How do they spend their
time? All of this information will help you to target
your book directly to your Ideal Customer.

But, I think that there's one more category of information that is the MOST important for precisely targeting your book topic and information – emotional information. Let's look at that now.

Emotional Information

Although this could properly be included in psychographic information, I like to separately identify my target market's emotional information. This includes their fears, pain, hopes and dreams – in that order.

If you know what keeps them up at night, and what transformation they're trying to achieve, you can target this emotional information with the topic of your book and with the individual chapters and information that you provide in those chapters.

To show you how to do this, I'm going to borrow heavily from GKIC. GKIC is a wonderful organization devoted to helping entrepreneurs succeed in business. I've been a member of GKIC for many years, and have built my law firm on the marketing lessons that I learned from them.

Identify Your Customer's Key Problem

First, identify your Ideal Customer's KEY PROBLEM – as it relates to your services or products. To do this, think about this question and how your Ideal Customer would respond:

If I Could Just _____.

The answers might look like this:

If I Could Just …

- Solve my tax problems, once and for all.

- Get a divorce without destroying my children.

- Get whiter teeth so that I'm not afraid to smile.

- Lose the fat and keep it off for good.

- Feel sexy again.

You get the point. Knowing your Ideal Customer's fears and pain will help you to pick a topic and chapters for your book. Of course, this needs to relate to a service or product that you offer!

Name Three to Five Things That Cause the Key Problem

Now that you know your Ideal Customer's Key Problem, I want you to think about three to five things that cause that that Key Problem. While doing this, I want you to think about the profile of your Ideal Customer that you've developed so far.

So, for example, let's look at:

If I Could Just Solve My Tax Problems, Once and For All.

If my Ideal Customer is a 47-year old male attorney with a solo practice (he's the only attorney), things that might cause him to have individual tax problems could include:

I didn't make my estimated tax payments;
I didn't file my tax returns; and,
I didn't budget my money to include the required tax payments.

However, if my Ideal Customer is a 38-year old male owner of a pizza shop, the causes of his tax problems might be related to the pizza shop and include:

I didn't pay my payroll taxes;
I didn't file my tax returns;
I don't make enough money to pay the payroll taxes and the rent; and,
I don't know how to budget my money given my erratic cash flow.

Finally, what if my Ideal Customer is a 75-year old retired woman who receives a small pension and social security, but has a large retirement account. Her tax problems could include:

I didn't file my tax returns;
I didn't withhold the taxes when I withdrew retirement savings; and
My spouse handled the taxes and I didn't know there was a problem.

Do you see how it helps to precisely target your Ideal Customer BEFORE you think about their emotional issues and their Key Problem? The Key Problem will probably be very different based on the demographics and psychographics of different customers.

Therefore, the topic of your book, and the information that you provide in that book, may be very different depending on the demographics, psychographics and emotional makeup of your ideal client.

Describe the Overall Picture of Your Ideal Customer

Now that you have all the pieces, it's time to describe your Ideal Customer. You'll have a real sense of who your Ideal Customer is, and what motivates them. You'll know their pain triggers and their desires for the future. You'll know your Ideal Customer as well as you know your close friends – and maybe more than that!

Once you've completed the Overall Picture for your Ideal Customer, it's time to do one more thing – describe their Ultimate Transformation.

The Ultimate Transformation

Now that you have a good idea of your Ideal Customer's Overall Picture, I want you to think about their hopes and dreams and the ultimate transformation that they're trying to achieve.

The goal of your book should be to take your reader on a journey, starting with their Key Problem, and ending with the transformation that they're trying to achieve. If you understand that journey and the Ultimate Transformation that they're looking for, you can tailor your book directly to that journey and Ultimate Transformation.

Let me give you some examples of what an Ultimate Transformation might look like, using the same examples from above.

For my 47-year-old attorney, his Ultimate Transformation might look like this:

"My tax debt is completely paid, the tax liens have been withdrawn, my credit is great, I don't have to worry about certified mail letters filling my mail box, and my wife is talking to me again!"

For my 38-year-old pizza shop owner, his Ultimate Transformation might look like this:

"My payroll tax debt is completely paid and I'm current with my ongoing payroll taxes, the business credit is great again and I'm able to access new credit lines to open a new restaurant, and I don't have to worry that my door will be padlocked when I get to the shop."

For my 75-year-old retiree, her Ultimate Transformation might look like this:

"The IRS has stopped garnishing my Social Security income and I can finally afford to eat at a restaurant every once in a while, I can finally stop worrying that the IRS is going to take my house and put me in jail, and I'm so relaxed that I started taking yoga and I'm in the best shape of my life."

So, do you get the point? Different Ideal Customers have different key problems, pain-points and Ultimate Transformations. That's why you need to pinpoint your Ideal Customer BEFORE you attempt to pick a topic for your book, outline the chapters for the book, and create the content. The book could be very different, depending upon the demographics, psychographics, and emotional responses of your Ideal Customer.

So, now it's time for you to do some work. It is REALLY important that you actually do this. I know that you're already thinking that writing a book shouldn't be this technical or involved. But, if you actually do this work now, everything else will be easier.

You'll be able to pick the ideal topic very quickly and you'll be able to breeze through the chapters and organization of your book. You'll be able to write the book in record time. And, you'll be able to easily market yourself and your book with the information that you gather in this chapter. So – Do IT! You'll thank me later.

Chapter 5 – How to Pick
a Topic for Your Book

In this chapter, I'm going to tell you how to pick a topic for your book. You may already have the perfect topic in mind. If so, great. If not, I'm going to walk you through several techniques to help you pick the perfect topic to accomplish your goals.

When I decide to write a book, I always do it for one reason – to promote a particular service that I offer. In the future, I may want to write a great novel or do something for something that I'm passionate about. But, for now – I focus exclusively on writing books to promote my business. In this model, writing a book is simply marketing.

Using the book as a marketing tool for you and your business is really the goal. Although you can use everything that I'm going to teach you to write and publish books about anything – I intend to focus exclusively on using your book to increase your Authority, Celebrity and Expertise.

I want your Ideal Customer to chase you and beg you for help. When you're the Celebrity in your niche, you can command premium prices and your income will explode.

So, that's why I had you go through the exercise in the last chapter to determine your Ideal Customer and target market. I want you to use the book to attract your Ideal Customer to your business or practice. But, you need to FIRST determine

WHO your Ideal Customer is so that you can precisely target that Ideal Customer with your book.

Narrow vs. Broad

Now that you have that Ideal Customer in mind, it should be pretty easy to select the topic for your book, right? Well, not so fast.

When I created the Ideal Customer profile for *I Can't Pay the IRS*, I determined that my Ideal Customer for my tax resolution business is a 47-year-old attorney from Orlando, FL with a small law firm. His tax problems are caused by not paying his estimated tax payments and filing his tax returns.

So, it should be relatively easy for me to come up with a topic for my Ideal Customer. Something like "How Lawyers Solve Their IRS Tax Problems…Once and For All! The Complete Insider's Guide to Defeating the Estimated Tax Monster!

That COULD be a good strategy. But, in addition to identifying and describing your Ideal Customer, you need to determine if the market for that Ideal Customer is large enough to support your income goals.

It's great to work with ONLY Ideal Customers. But if there are only a handful of Ideal Customers in the geographic area that you serve – and that handful won't give you enough revenue to meet your income goals – then you need to think more broadly.

So, the first question before choosing a topic for your book is whether you can write your book directly to your Ideal Customer – and exclude every other potential customer. The answer may well be yes.

Because I can handle IRS tax resolution cases anywhere in the country, I COULD have easily focused the book precisely on my Ideal Customer and excluded every other customer. However, as I developed the tax practice, I decided that I wanted to start in my backyard – the counties surrounding Orlando, Florida.

My plan is to expand nationally. But, I wanted to get my systems in place before fully expanding into a national presence. This meant that there would NOT be enough attorneys with tax problems in my local area to meet my income goals.

As a result, I decided to expand the topic of the book to include not only my Ideal Customer, but other types of customers as well. This does NOT mean that I completely discounted all the work that I did in identifying my Ideal Customer. Instead, I just expanded his particular concerns to include concerns that other clients with tax problems might have.

I STILL spoke to my Ideal Customer throughout the book. But, I also spoke to other potential clients as well.

So, you need to first go through this analysis as well. Now that you've identified your Ideal Customer, can you write your book DIRECTLY to that Ideal Customer and exclude all other potential clients or customers. Is the market that you serve large enough for you to make enough money with this laser focus?

If the answer is yes, then you SHOULD choose the narrow focus for your book topic and chapters. It will be much easier for you to become a Celebrity in a smaller niche than in a larger niche.

However, if you're like me, and you don't think that you can make enough income by focusing exclusively on your Ideal Customer, then broaden the focus of your book to INCLUDE your Ideal Customer, but other clients and customers as well.

If you write a book this time that includes more than your Ideal Customer, you may decide that you're going to write a narrow book next time that will focus exclusively on your Ideal Customer.

I may do that for my next book. In fact, I have several books in mind that will focus exclusively on different types on clients, including my Ideal Customer.

So, with that in mind, I want you to think about your practice or business and decide what topic will give you the most Authority, Celebrity and Expertise and the most bang for your buck. You can ultimately write several books like I've done to promote different parts of your practice or business. But, for now, let's focus on one.

Let me give you some examples. Let's say that you're an attorney that specializes in probate and trusts. If your Ideal Customer is a 56-year-old white collar worker in your geographic area, you may want to go narrow and write a book on "White Collar Secrets for Avoiding Probate."

Or, you may want to broaden the focus to include other customers and write a book on "The Secrets that Everyone Needs to Know to Avoid Probate." (These aren't great titles. We'll talk about how to create the perfect title and Subtitles in a later chapter.)

Or, maybe you're a massage therapist that wants to promote a particular form of massage. Your Ideal Customer is a 42-year-old stay-at-home mother that you think could benefit from that form of massage. You could write a book titled "The Secret Massage for Mothers. How Mothers Look and Feel Younger and Sexier With Healing Touch."

Or, you could broaden the focus with "The Secret Massage. How to Look and Feel Younger and Sexier With Healing Touch." You could also write a book to promote certain supplements that you offer to your clients – or combine the topics.

Or, maybe you're a doctor that specializes in preventative, anti-aging, and hormone replacement therapy. Your Ideal Customer is a 55-year-old woman who is recently divorced and wants to start dating again. Your book could be "Don't Let Your Body Slow You Down! The Divorcee's Guide to Choosing the Body You Want With Natural Hormone Replacement."

Or, you could broaden the focus with "Don't Let Your Body Slow You Down! The Ultimate Guide to Choosing the Body You Want With Natural Hormone Replacement." You could write a book on any one of your areas of practice and also focus on specific supplements and treatments that you offer.

Using Amazon as a Research Tool

If you're stuck on what to write about, go to Amazon and enter some terms associated with the service that you want to promote. Amazon is a great research tool for coming up with ideas for your book and also for researching subject matter to include in your books.

It's also good to read the reviews on similar books to see what readers DIDN'T like about these books. You may want to include this information in your book – more on this later.

I also don't want you to get discouraged if you see several books that are EXACTLY like the book that you want to create. Remember, we're not trying to make you rich selling books on Amazon. We're trying to establish your Authority, Celebrity and Expertise and increase your income by providing the services that you promote in your book.

So, it doesn't matter how many books are exactly like your book on Amazon. If anything, this may indicate that your instincts are correct and there's a market for your book in the world. So, many similar books may actually be a good thing.

Forums

Another option for picking a topic is to review forums for the niche that you want to conquer. There are forums for practically anything. I'm constantly amazed at the wide range of things that people are interested in.

So, how do you use a forum to pick a topic? Simply enter your niche, or the service or product you want to promote, and the word "forum" in a Google search. So, for example, if a dentist wants to promote her teeth whitening business, she would search for "teeth whitening forum." And yes, there are many forums for this.

When you find a forum for the service or product, look at the comments from the people in the forum. What are they interested in? What concerns them? What information are they looking for? All of this should help you to identify the problems that they have and how you can help them to solve those problems. With that information, you should be able to pick a topic for your book.

Freewriting

If you're still stuck on what your book should be about, another way to pull it out of you is to do an exercise called freewriting. In freewriting, you just start writing anything and everything that comes to mind about your book.

Give yourself 5 minutes – yes actually time it – and start writing. Don't worry about what comes out or how it sounds. Just keep going. Don't stop until the time runs out. Let me give you some thoughts to get you started:

> I want to write a book because …..
> I want to make sure that everyone knows I offer …
> I want to teach people how to …
> I want to make more money from …

These are just some ideas. Sometimes when we write, we're our own worst enemy. Freewriting is a way to stop thinking and to set your mind free. Your mind actually knows what it wants and needs to write about. You just have to give it permission to do it!

Don't discount freewriting until you've tried it. If you can't come up with a topic for your book, let your mind run free with freewriting. You'll be amazed with the results!

Ask Your Clients or Customers

Another way to come up with a topic for your book is to simply ask your clients, customers or prospects what they want to know about and are interested in receiving from you. You may be surprised at the responses that you receive and you might get some ideas for new services or products that you never thought about.

So, how do you do this? There are several ways.

The easiest way to do this is to create several questions that you want your target audience to respond to and send it by email or mail. For example, let's say that you're a CPA and want to increase your revenue from small business clients. But, you don't know what these clients want or need from you. So, you might create the following questions:

Are you happy with your current CPA?

Are there any services that you wish your CPA offered but doesn't? Or, are there any services that you wish I offered but don't?

What information would help your business grow?

What challenges do you have in running your business?

If you could waive a magic wand and fix anything in your business, what would it be?

You could build a more detailed set of questions. But, don't do too much. You want the target to actually answer the questions. If there are too many, you won't get any responses.

You can also create a survey using any of the many on-line tools for doing this. For example, a service called "Survey Monkey" will allow you to send a list of your questions to several people for free.

You can also sign up for a more involved service for a very low monthly cost. There are other services that offer a similar product, such as LeadQuizzes.com.

With any of these services, you can send the questionnaires to your existing clients by email, or you can post the quiz on your web page, or post the quiz on Facebook. You can also use the quiz as a lead generation tool with Facebook ads and using lists. But, for now, let's keep it simple.

I hope this has given you some ideas on how to create the topic for your book. By now, you should have the topic in mind. Now, we need to focus on writing your rough draft. Let's do that next.

Section 3 - Write Your Rough Draft – FAST!

Most people never write the book that they know they need to write because they think it will take too long. The thought of sitting at a computer and typing away for days on end isn't very appealing. But, it really doesn't have to work like that.

In this section, I'm going to show you my secrets for writing fast. And, the basic formula looks like this:

1. Mind Map Your Book

2. Use the Mind Map to Create an Outline

3. Mind Map Your Individual Chapters

4. Complete the Outline

5. Use the Outline to Complete Your Rough Draft

So, let's look the steps of my basic formula and some of the secrets for making the process fast and painless!

Chapter 6: Use Mind Maps to Create a Strong Outline

The first step – and this is a REAL secret – is to mind map your book and the individual chapters. You know, we're all taught in school to start with an outline and then write your paper. Right?

But, how many times have you stared at a blank piece of paper or empty computer monitor trying to create an outline? Many times, I would just start writing because I couldn't create an outline. In school, when we were required to turn in an outline, I would usually write the paper and THEN create the outline to turn in – because I hated writing outlines.

Now, this is NOT the most efficient way to write. But, I eventually discovered a secret for creating an outline and for increasing my writing speed by 10 times - it's called "Mind Mapping."

Step 1 – Create a Mind Map

A Mind Map is essentially a brain-dump of everything you know or want to know about your project. To write a book, you start with a central theme – typically the book topic, and spread out from there.

I've experimented with mind mapping for years. There are many computer programs that have been developed to help you create mind maps. And, I've tried a lot of them. But, I find that I get lost in the process of trying to use the software and miss the point of mind mapping which is to brain-dump. So, I create mind maps by hand instead.

How to Create a Mind Map

To create a mind map, you start with a blank sheet of paper, poster board, or a white board. You start with the center of the paper or white board, and place your central idea – your book topic.

From that center topic, you start drawing bubble thoughts out all around to represent different ideas about the topic. This should include anything and everything that you can think of regarding the topic – points you want to make, stories you want to tell, ideas you want to convey.

Don't stop until you've gotten everything out of your brain. Don't worry about the way it looks.

All that matters is that you're trying to free your brain to write down everything that it knows – or wants to know – about that topic.

Start With the Problems

I usually start by thinking about the problems that my Ideal Customer has. The real point of your book should be to bring your client down a path from where they are now, to the ultimate transformation that they want to achieve.

So, I start with the problems that they have now to show them where they are now. And, you want to write down everything that you can think about relating to their problems. There may be several problems, or there may be one, with related problems. Whatever it is, you just need to get it out of your brain and onto the paper or whiteboard.

Then Brainstorm Solutions

Next, you may want to start brainstorming solutions. What services can you offer to your client that will solve their problems and allow them to get to their ultimate transformation? Write down everything that comes to mind.

Think About Stories

What about stories? I think that you should weave stories throughout your book. People love stories. So, while you're brainstorming, think if there are any stories that you can add to your book, either to illustrate a point that you want to make, or to show some successes that you've have with your clients.

So, continue to write down anything and everything that you can think of about your book topic. Don't stop, just write. Remember, the point of the mind mapping is to free your mind. You may be surprised at how much you know when you free your mind – so let it run free.

Step 2 – Use the Mind Map to Create an Outline

Once you've completed your brain dump and created the mind map, it's time to turn that mind map into the chapters and sub-chapters in your book. All that you need to do is transfer the information from the mind map into a traditional outline. This will be really easy because you've already done the heavy lifting with the mind map. The outline will almost write itself.

Take the common themes from your mind map and organize them into sections. So, for example, let's say that you identified three problems that your Ideal Customer may currently have. You could organize each of those problems into chapters and sub-chapters.

Then, maybe you identified five solutions to help your Ideal Customer solve their problems and achieve the ultimate transformation that they want to achieve. You could make each of those solutions a chapter in your book with sub-chapters.

As you do this, you may find other things that should go into the outline. That's OK. Just add it in. You want the outline to be as detailed as possible. And, using the mind map to outline process will really help to make this easy.

Step 3 – Mind Map the Individual Chapters

Once you've created the outline to include the chapters, you should then create a mind map for each individual chapter. This will help you to identify the sub-chapters and additional content for each chapter.

To do this, just repeat the same process as before. Start with the chapter topic in the center of the mind map. Then, start brainstorming everything that you want to tell the reader about that chapter.

Although you may have identified some chapter information in your initial mind map of the entire book, you will probably find that it's now easier to identify much more information for each chapter when you focus only on that chapter with a mind map. Try it. You'll thank me later!

Step 4 – Complete the Outline

Once you've completed a mind map for each individual chapter, just add that additional information into your outline. As before, you'll see the natural patterns emerge from the mind map. Sections and sub-chapters will naturally group and be obvious to you. Just take those sections and sub-chapters and fit them into the outline.

When you're done, you're going to have a strong outline that will make writing your rough draft a breeze! You won't be staring at a blank piece of paper or empty monitor. You'll know exactly what you need to say and when.

Step 5 – Use the Outline to Create the Rough Draft

Now that you have a detailed outline for your book, it's time to write the rough draft. I can hear you moaning from here! Don't worry, I told you that I'm going to make this easy. In the next chapter, I'm going to show you several ways to get your rough draft done - FAST – and most don't require that you type anything.

(If you want to see how the Mind Map process works, you can watch one of the training videos from my premium training program, *Publishing Hacks*. You can find that video, and several other free resources at www.UpYourACE.com/resources.)

Chapter 7: How to Write Fast – Even if You're Not a Good Writer and Hate to Write

OK. We've hit the part of the course that you've been waiting for. But, if you've done the research and the brainstorming, it will be much easier than you think to actually write the book.

There are many different techniques for doing the actual writing. I'm going to talk to you about six of those techniques. I've used every one of them over the years, so I can give you a good idea of the pros and cons of each.

Method #1 - Crank It Out

Once you have your chapters in order and an outline, you can simply start typing! I almost always do this at some point – regardless of any other method that I start with.

I just start writing. I don't worry too much at this point about grammar or style. I just write. It's not quite freewriting, but I'm not stopping to edit, either.

If you feel comfortable typing, you can certainly crank it out.

However, with that said. This is probably the slowest of the techniques that I'll talk about in this chapter. If speed is your primary concern, you may want to try one of the other techniques that I'm going to discuss.

Method #2 - Dictate and Transcribe

Whenever I talk to people about writing a book, they typically tell me that they're not good writers, or that they don't have time to write a book.

I'll usually respond by asking them if they know the subject area that they want to write about. They'll say "Of Course. I've been doing this for 20 years!" So, I'll ask them "If I asked you about the basic questions that someone needing your services or product has, can you tell me the answers?"

The answer is "Of course." I could talk about it all day." Bingo! Most of you REALLY know the subject matter of the book that you want to write about. In fact, if I put you in front of your prospects, you could go on and on about the subject, and never take a breath.

So, let's use that to write a book. Instead of TYPING your book – SPEAK it. That's right, just start talking your book.

Dictate It!

Now, to do this, you still need your organization and chapter outline that you developed earlier. Then, just start talking about the chapters and the sub-chapters. Don't worry about how you sound, or worry if you make a mistake. Just keep talking!

So, you're probably wondering – "How do I record what I'm saying?" Well, there are many ways to do this.

The easiest way to do this is to use your smart phone. Use the record feature and start talking. You can also use your computer. PC's and Macs come standard with the ability to record. You should also consider using Audacity – which is a free program that has more editing functions than the recorders that come standard on your computer.

Transcribe It

So, once you've recorded your chapters, now what do you do? Now, you need someone to transcribe the audio recording. So, let's talk about several ways to do this.

Fiverr.com

One of the easiest ways to do this is to find someone on Fiverr. Fiverr is one of my favorite tools for getting all sorts of stuff done inexpensively.

If you've never heard of Fiverr, I guarantee that you're going to get hooked looking through the site once you see it. Fiverr offers any number of services for $5. Fiverr calls these services "Gigs." I used Fiverr to create my last book cover. I've also used it for logo design, marketing assistance, and ... transcription services.

As I write this book, you can get 30 minutes of audio transcribed for $5 on Fiverr. So, let's do the math. My last book was 107 pages long – what I believe to be in the range of a perfect book for our purposes. There are 23,260 words in the entire book. The average person can speak about 110-150 words per minute. So, let's say that we're on the low end, and are speaking really slow – or 110 words per minute.

It would take 211.45 minutes of recording to dictate an entire book. Therefore, if you're paying $5 per 30 minutes to transcribe the book, it will cost you under $40 to have the entire book transcribed!! That's pretty incredible if you think about it. I love Fiverr!

To use Fiverr for transcribing, you just need to create a Fiverr account, then follow the directions from the service provider. They'll direct you to upload the audio file directly to Fiverr. And, they'll take it from there.

Upwork.com

Another option that you may want to consider for transcribing your book is Upwork. I've used Upwork (or its predecessor Elance) for many projects. Let's look at Upwork.

As you can see, you can hire someone to do your transcription work on Upwork just as you can on Fiverr. The price tends to run higher - typically

$30/hour – or about three times the cost of Fiverr. But, you may want to experiment with different transcription service providers and see if one works better for you. Even with the higher fees at Upwork, it would still cost less than $120 to get your entire book transcribed!

As with Fiverr, you need to set up an account with UpWork and then follow the service provider's instructions. They will ask you to upload the audio file and you're good to go.

Rev App

Another Option is to use the Rev App. You can download the Rev app to your smart phone and record your voice directly to the app. You can then request that Rev transcribe the audio that you recorded into their app. With Rev, you don't need to upload anything. You just push the button in the app and you're good to go.

The only problem with Rev is that it costs $1 per minute of audio – or about 6 times more expensive than Fiverr. So, you'll pay just under $215 for the transcription that we just reviewed.

Dictate and Transcribe It Yourself

Another variation of the record and transcribe method is to simply do the transcription yourself. You can do this one of two ways. First, you can literally type the words while listening to your voice recording. If you're comfortable typing, this can be a great way to complete the transcription.

But, you're probably wondering why you would do this? Why not just type it in the first place? Because, the value of the recording is the speaking.

It's MUCH easier for most people to talk about something than it is to write about it. That's why I suggest that you record you talking about the book, rather than cranking it out. It's still much easier to type what you've already said.

You can also use a voice transcription program – like Dragon - to transcribe your audio. There are also apps for your phone – or that even come free with your phone – that will do this as well.

Although you CAN do the transcription yourself, I'm not a fan. I'd rather pay someone $40 to transcribe my audio and include all of the punctuation, etc. I've found that professional transcribers are also generally better at getting more of the words correct. But, if you want to get the book done as cheaply as possible, you can transcribe it yourself.

Method #3 - Interview and Transcribe

A variation of the record and transcribe model is to have someone interview you while recording the video. This will probably provide a more realistic sound to your book, because you're actually responding to someone asking you questions.

To do this, you need to develop questions for your "interviewer" to ask you. You should get those questions from the exercises that we did earlier. For each chapter, and each sub-chapter, ask and answer the questions that your reader/prospect REALLY wants to know. You know what they are. This can be a very effective technique if you craft the questions correctly.

Once you have the audio, just use any of the techniques that we talked about above to get it transcribed.

Method #4 -Present and Transcribe

Another variation of the record and transcribe model is to give a presentation and record it – either by video or audio - and transcribe the recording. I try to give presentations as often as possible, and almost always videotape the presentation. This is a great way by itself to establish your Authority, Celebrity and Expertise, both with the audience that you're addressing and with subsequent viewers who see you giving a presentation to an audience. People naturally assume that you're an authority and expert because you're giving a presentation.

Apart from this, however, it's a great way to get the contents for your book. I used this method – along with the ghost writer method I'm going to talk about in the next segment – to write my third book. If you feel comfortable giving presentations

– and even if you don't – try this method to write your book. It's very powerful.

Once you have the recording, simply send it to a transcriber as we discussed in the previous sections.

Method #5 – Use a Ghost Writer

Really? Ghost writer? Isn't that expensive? No. Isn't that dishonest? No.

To write my third book, *Save Your Florida Home ... Now! Or Walk Away With No Debt, Better Credit and Money in Your Pocket*, I gave a presentation to a group of homeowners about foreclosure defense. I had the presentation recorded and then sent the recording to a ghost writer and told him to write a book based on my presentation.

He came back with a book that was about 65 pages long and charged me about $800 for the service. Now, I could have simply sent the recording to a transcription service and had it transcribed – and it would have been much cheaper as we've seen.

But, by sending it to the ghost writer, I received a polished book that was in my OWN voice because I said everything. The ghost writer filled in a lot of blanks and did his own research to do this. It was worth every penny that I paid him for this.

However, I wanted a book that was more substantial than 65 pages. So, I started to crank out the rest of the book.

The book ended up being 299 pages long (Way too long for our purposes, but that's what happened.) But, it took me a fraction of the time that it might have taken otherwise because the ghostwriter gave me the organizational structure for the book – and I just added to it.

Do I think that hiring a ghostwriter is dishonest? Nope! I wish that I could have been happy with the 65-page book and NOT have written all the rest of it. The book WAS my writing because it came from my presentation. The ghostwriter just polished it up for me.

So, if you give presentations, or think that you might want to do this, think about hiring a ghostwriter. A ghostwriter WILL do the WHOLE book for you – even without a recording. And, you can do this. I like to do it myself. But, if you don't, who am I to judge?

So, how do you hire a ghostwriter? I would start with UpWork. Type in "ghostwriter" and look at the reviews. I would try to find someone who has written in your area. I would also request a fixed rate for the total job.

Final Thoughts About Writing the Rough Draft

Just Do It! Just start writing – or talking!

I know, it sounds so easy when I describe the process. But then your brain kicks in with all the fears – it will take too long, I can't write, I'm not really an expert, I'm not certified, I don't have all the research, people won't want to read what I write …

Don't listen to your fears. Just start. Don't worry what it looks like or how it sounds. The rough draft is called the rough draft for a reason. You're going to clean it up later.

Section 4 - Finish Your Book - Make It Look Like a Real Book

I told you earlier that your book needs to look like a "real" book – one that you could find on any bookstore shelf. I've seen too many self-published books that look like self-published books. That instantly diminishes their value to the author.

So, what are the things that will immediately identify your book as a cheap knock-off? The list is long but includes a bad title, a poorly designed cover, no editing, no interior typesetting, and not including the additional sections that are included in all books produced by traditional publishing houses.

So, in this section, I'm going to briefly discuss all of these things and show you how to avoid the mistakes.

CHAPTER 8: CRAFT THE PERFECT TITLE AND SUBTITLE FOR YOUR BOOK

The very next thing for you to consider is your title and subtitle. Does it seem strange that we're just now talking about the title and subtitle?

There are many experts that advise you to select your book title even before you start to write. Although I generally have some working title in mind when I start to write, I almost always change that title later.

This is generally because I have a much stronger idea of the book after I've actually completed the first draft than before I start. I think that you'll find this is true for you as well.

So, I like to create the actual title and subtitle AFTER I write the rough draft. That's why we're just talking about it now.

Your book title is probably the most important part of your book – perhaps as important as the actual contents of the book. Why?

Many people may never actually read your book. But, they can at least read the title and can make the mental decision that you're THE Authority, Celebrity and Expert on a topic that they're interested in or concerned about.

So, let's look at the process for creating that perfect title and subtitle. When I create a title, I follow a few basic rules to do so.

Start with a Transformation in Mind

Your reader wants to know how to solve a problem that they have. You should be writing to a particular reader who has a particular problem. They're looking for the transformation. Your title should promise the transformation.

So, for example, in my book to promote my tax resolution business, the title is *"I Can't Pay the IRS ... Now What? The Ultimate Insider's Guide to Solving Your Tax Problems – Once and For All!"* So, the book is targeted to people who have tax problems and are looking to solve them. The promise of transformation is to solve their tax problems – once and for all.

How about the title of this book - *"If You're Not a Celebrity, You're a Commodity! How to Use the Secret of Celebrity to Attract New Customers and Obliterate Your Competition!"* So, although implied, the book is targeted to people who are struggling to attract customers and compete in their niche. The promise of transformation is that by using the secret of celebrity, they will be able to attract new customers and not only compete in their niche, but actually obliterate their completion! Cool. Right?

Make the Title Attention-Grabbing

This should be obvious. But, it's important. I tried to make the title to this book attention-grabbing by being controversial. People may argue that my title "If You're Not a Celebrity ... You're a Commodity" isn't necessarily true. I know – you can NOT be a celebrity and still have a thriving business.

I don't care. The message is sound, and professionals and small business owners need to think outside the box to get noticed in a sea of competition. And, the title is attention-grabbing and starts a conversation. That's what a good title should do.

Make it Clear What the Book is About

Your book title should make it clear what your book is about. Don't be creative at the expense of clarity. You want your reader to fully understand what the book is about and how it can help them. I've seen too many book titles that were so cryptic that the target audience would never even look at the book because they wouldn't realize it was intended for them.

Don't fall in the trap of trying to be so clever that you miss the target audience completely. I came close to being too clever with the title of this book. Standing alone, the target audience would never know that the book was for them or what it was about.

So, if you DO want to be clever with the title, just make sure the subtitle saves the day by describing who the book is for and what the transformation is for the target audience. I believe that I accomplished this with the subtitle to this book!

The Title Should be Short and Memorable, But the Subtitle Should be More Descriptive

See my title again. Enough said.

How to Pick the Actual Title

For me, when I find the right title – I know it. Hopefully, that will be the same for you. However, if you can't seem to settle on one title from several, let other people help you. Ideally, you should let your target market select the title for you.

You could use the title selection process as an early marketing effort for your book. Send out emails to your current clients or customers. Let them know that you're writing a book and are trying to select the title. Ask them to vote on the title. By doing this, you'll get a sense of what your target audience thinks about the title, and you'll start to get a buzz about your book in the market. You can also do this through Facebook or LinkedIn or as a promotion for clients or customers that come into your office or store.

Final Thoughts About Your Title and Subtitle

I want to emphasize again the importance of the Title and Subtitle. I truly believe that most people won't actually read your entire book. But, if you craft the Title and Subtitle perfectly for your target audience, it won't matter whether they read your book or not.

They'll see the title and subtitle, self-identify as a target for your book, see that you wrote the book, and determine that you're THE Authority, Celebrity, and Expert on that topic. Then, they'll chase you to solve their problems and help them achieve their ultimate transformation.

But, you still need to make your book look like a book. You can't just have a great title and subtitle on a crappy book! So, once you have your title selected, it's time to add the additional sections to your book that every "real" book should contain. Let's look at those now.

CHAPTER 9: CREATE THE ADDITIONAL SECTIONS OF YOUR BOOK

As I've said many times before, your book needs to look like a "real" book. This means that it must contain the additional sections that are included in all books published by traditional publishers. Therefore, your book should contain the following sections in addition to the actual content:

Title Page
Copyright and Legal Stuff Page
Product, Sales Pitch or Lead Capture Page
Table of Contents
Acknowledgements Page
Introduction
Conclusion

In this chapter, I'm going to briefly discuss each section. If you want to see what they look like, just see how I did it for this book!

Title Page

The Title Page just contains the Title, the Subtitle and the Author's Name.

Copyright and Legal Stuff Page

Copyright is a form of protection to the authors of "original works of authorship." It gives the author exclusive right to reproduce copies of the book, create derivative works of the book, to sell the book, etc.

Under current law, you do NOT need to register the book with the United States Copyright Office to get the protection of copyright. You don't even need to list the copyright in your book as I'm getting ready to show you.

But, you want your book to look just like any other book in the bookstore or library. Therefore, you should include a copyright page in your book.

The copyright notice should contain three things:

The symbol © or the word copyright;
The year of first publication of the book and subsequent publication dates; and,
The name of the owner of the copyright.

If you look at the copyright page from this book, you'll see all of these elements. I always like to update the date of publication when I can to make the book seems as new as possible. You should consider doing this as well. Readers are more likely to be impressed with your book if the information is a recent as possible.

Liability Disclaimer

If you're a professional offering advice, it's probably best to add a liability disclaimer to your book. It's amazing what people can blame you for based on your "advice."

It seems crazy that you should have to tell people that you're not giving accounting advice when you're a lawyer or vice versa, but that's just how it is. Take a look at the liability disclaimer that I included in this book and feel free to use it as is or to modify it according to your needs.

Contact Information

You want to make sure that people know how to contact you. Remember, the whole point of the book is to make a sale of your product or services. Your potential clients or customers won't be able to find you if you don't tell them how to do this. I like to do it at the very beginning and at the very end, at least.

Product, Sales Pitch or Lead Capture Page

You probably won't find this page in most books – but you should. Remember, the whole point of the book is to sell your product or service. Although I'm not a fan of making the book one long sales pitch, I do think that it's important to weave a sales message in throughout the book.

The product or sales pitch page is one of those places to do this. In *I Can't Pay the IRS*, I put a pitch for my IRS1099 app. The app allows prospects to review videos and ask me specific questions about tax resolution. They can also send me a picture of any IRS notices that they receive. The app allows for more engagement with my prospects and I use it frequently as a lead magnet.

You can also see what I did in this book. I'm promoting several of my training programs, including *Publishing Hacks*, my ongoing training, and my Done-With-You services.

You could use almost anything on this page. You can include an offer for a free, or reduced-price service or product. You could offer a free 4-part video series relevant to the topic of the book. You would then capture their email address and could start marketing to them with an autoresponder sequence.

Or, you could just have a very simple call to action, like call my office or store for a free consultation. (This isn't the strongest offer in the world). But, you get the point.

Don't lose the opportunity to make a sale by forgoing this page. I've made a great deal of money from people who responded to the Sales Pitch page in my books. You can, too.

Table of Contents

Remember, you want your book to look just like the books in the book store. This means that you need a table of contents. It doesn't really matter how you break down the topics.

Personally, I like to include as much in the Table of Contents as possible. This means that I generally include not only the chapter headings, but all of the subchapter headings as well. I like to make it easy for people to find information in the book.

Also, since I believe that most people won't actually read your book in its entirety, I think it's important that they can look at your Table of Contents to be able to go directly to the information that they're looking for, or to at least be awed by the amount of information that is included in your book. A very detailed Table of Contents will accomplish this.

How do you create a Table of Contents? If you're writing your book with Word – and I assume that this is the case – just use the Table of Contents creator in Word. It will produce a very nice Table of Contents for you.

Acknowledgements Page

I always like to include an Acknowledgements page in all my books. It's important to recognize and thank the people in your life that have helped you in general and specifically in writing your book. The number of people that I've thanked has varied over my books.

In this book, I had several acknowledgements. The first was my wife – that's always smart – and true.

The next was my family for putting up with me while I focused on creating my courses and this book.

The next acknowledgement was to the many mentors who have shaped my understanding of marketing. I acknowledged them because they really have helped me to get to where I am today. I also want to plant a seed that EVERYONE needs mentors – including the reader.

The next acknowledgement was for my personal coaching students. Again, I really am thankful to my students. But, I'm also planting another seed here. I want readers to understand that I accept private clients.

The final acknowledgment was to "the thousands of clients who have entrusted me with their financial lives throughout the years." Although this was true, it was also a marketing message. I wanted to emphasize that I've helped thousands of clients … over the years. So, it shows experience in both numbers of clients and years.

Now, I don't think that you always need to add in marketing pitches into your Acknowledgement page – but it never hurts.

The bottom line with this page – be sincere and thank the people that have impacted your life. It feels good to do it, and the subjects of your acknowledgement will be touched. It's a win-win.

Introduction

The Introduction is meant to tell the reader what the book is about and to encourage them to read the book. As I've mentioned before, many readers may only skim the Title Page, the Table of Contents, and the Introduction. So, you want to make the Introduction good so that they understand what you're offering. You also want them to

WANT to read the book. Hopefully, the Introduction will do this.

Many people who teach aspiring authors how to write a book, suggest that they write the Introduction BEFORE they write the first draft. I've always had a problem with that.

Frequently, even with a strong outline, my rough draft varies from what I thought it was going to be before I start to write it. So, I like the book to develop FIRST, before I write the Introduction.

This is just my personal preference. You could write the Introduction first and edit it after you've completed the book – that's up to you.

I use a basic formula for drafting the Introduction. The format that I'm using now came from my friends at GKIC – I mentioned them already. Here it is:

> State your Name
> Tell Your Story
> This book is for [Target Prospect] who wants to [Solve Key Challenge]
> Let's Get Started [Call to Action]

This doesn't need to be difficult. Just follow the formula. Look at the introduction to this book. I told the reader my name. I told them my story – weaving in an explanation of my extensive experience. I also told the readers about my own challenges.

I think it's important to always show your reader that you're human. If you don't do this, they won't believe that they can do it, too. Sure, I can do these things because I'm an attorney, etc. How can they do it? I show them that I am as flawed as they are – and maybe more.

I learned this technique from several of my mentors, including Joel Bauer, Suzanne Evans and Larry Winget. They all teach professional speakers that they should first build themselves up, and then tear themselves down, so that people can relate to them.

I also use this technique in all of my marketing efforts. I believe that it is responsible for much of my financial success – along with my books. Many of my clients have told me that they hired me specifically because "I'd been there – like them – and wouldn't look down on them because of that."

Think about this when you're writing the Introduction. You want to build yourself up for the A.C.E. – Authority, Credibility and Expertise – but then tear yourself down to be human and to relate to your readers – your prospects. This can be very powerful.

This Book is For … The next part of the formula is whom this book is for. You can see how I used this part of the formula at the end of the Introduction to this book. The point is to let your reader self-identify with the book. You want them to say "Yeah. That's me!"

Finally, my Call to Action was "So, if you're ready to change your life, let's go!" Pretty simple.

If you follow this straightforward process, you'll be able to complete your Introduction very quickly. Just get it done!

Conclusion

The final section of the book is your Conclusion. As with the individual chapters, I like to follow the basic format of tell them what you're going to tell them, tell them, and tell them what you told them. In the broader sense, the Introduction is the "tell them what you're going to tell them," the chapters are the "tell them," and the Conclusion is the "tell them what you told them."

I also like to use the Conclusion as one more opportunity to get my sales message and contact information out to the reader.

If you look at the Conclusion in this book, you can see that I did many things.

First, I gave an overall message about the book. Then, I told the reader that they CAN write a book by following the steps in this book. But, if they want to do it FAST and EASY, they should enroll in one of my courses.

Then, I reminded the reader that there are MANY ways to use their book to establish themselves as THE Authority, Celebrity and Expert in their niche. Therefore, they will benefit from enrolling in my ongoing training to learn all of the techniques.

Then, I gave the reader contact information and told them that I take a limited number of new private clients. I told the reader this to establish a sense of limited availability and as a form of "takeaway selling." I want the reader to beg me to coach them – and not the other way around. (Of course, to a large degree, this is true. I do have limited availability for private clients!)

So, as you can see, I've been able to pack a lot into the Conclusion section. This also goes to my belief that many people don't read the whole book. They may only read the Title, the Table of Contents, the Introduction, and the Conclusion.

Therefore, I want each of those sections to accomplish the marketing goal for which they were intended – to get the reader to become a client or customer. This should be your goal as well.

Final Thoughts About the Additional Sections

I hope that you see the value of having the "additional sections" in your book. First, having them in the book makes the book look like a "real" book that you could find on a bookstore shelf. But, you can see that most of the sections also help to promote you as the Authority, Celebrity, and Expert in your niche and provide opportunities for direct sales pitches to your readers!

CHAPTER 10: EDIT YOUR BOOK

No matter how good you are as a writer, you're going to need to edit your work. If you followed my advice and didn't edit as you wrote, it's now time to do the editing.

Read Your Book Out Loud First

Before you have someone else read your book for edits, I would suggest that you read the entire book out loud. I've done this with all of my books and it really helps to make the book SOUND right.

I told you before that I want to write like I talk. There's no better way to do this than to read your book out loud. You'll find that you catch a lot of problems with this read through.

Once you've done this, it's best to have SOMEONE ELSE edit the book – not you. I've found that by the time I complete a book, I'm too close to the words to see the flaws. When someone else points them out to me – it's obvious. But before that, I might have read a particular passage 20 times and never seen the mistake. So, let someone else do the editing.

So, let's talk about editing. There are essentially four types of editing – sometimes these are lumped together.

Big Picture Editing

Also called substantive, developmental or structural editing. This involves the overall structure of the book and how everything fits together. This could involve moving sections of the book around, adding sections, or dropping sections.

Paragraph Level Editing

Also called stylistic or line editing. This involves recasting sentences for clarity, flow and rhythm. Are your sentences clear, fluid and pleasurable to read?

Sentence Level Editing

Also called copyediting. This involves grammar, usage and consistency issues.

Word Level Editing

Also called proofreading. This involves typos, repeated words, spelling, punctuation and formatting issues.

How to Find an Editor

Ask a Talented Family Member or Friend

I've been blessed with two wives that were/are both brilliant writers. (My first wife passed away from cancer). They acted as my editors for four of my five books. We often disagreed about the edits, but I ALMOST always went with their suggestions. (I used a professional editor for the second book)

If you have someone in your life that is a good writer and you trust, you certainly can have them edit your book for you. This is typically the cheapest way to go, and depending on your relationship with your "editor," also the fastest way to go.

Hire a Professional Editor

But, if you're not blessed with a brilliant writer in your circle of family or friends, you'll need to hire a professional editor.

There are several ways to do this:

Fiverr

First, you can search on Fiverr. We talked about Fiverr earlier in the book when we discussed transcribing services. I love Fiverr! Just go to www.Fiverr.com. And enter the search term "book editing."

You'll see multiple people offering their editing services. The amount varies, but the going rate seems to be about $5.00+ per 1,000 words. *I Can't Pay the IRS* has 23,260 words – a 117-page book. So, it would cost you approximately $100 – or a little more – to have a 117-page book edited – not too bad.

If you're going to go this route, make sure that you look at the number of reviews and the quality of the reviews before you select an editor. You can also typically pay more to get the job completed more quickly.

Upwork

Another option that we've also discussed is Upwork – which used to be Elance. You can search Upwork just like you did with Fiverr. However, to actually hire someone through Upwork, you'll need to create a free account and submit a post. Freelance editors will bid on your proposal.

As we discussed before, the rates are likely to be higher on Upwork than on Fiverr. You'll probably end up paying $300 - $600 for a book the size of *I Can't Pay the IRS* – 117 pages.

CreateSpace

Another option is CreateSpace. We're going to talk about CreateSpace in great detail when we discuss actually publishing your book. For now, however, let's just talk about the editing services that CreateSpace offers.

CreateSpace lumps editing into two categories – line editing and copyediting.

Line Editing – CreateSpace describes its Line Editing Service as "a professional editor will review your manuscript and provide recommendations for improving the structure and flow, as well as review for consistency in grammar, spelling, and punctuation."

CreateSpace charges $210 up to 10,000 words, and $.021 per word over 10,000 words. So, for *I Can't Pay the IRS*, the cost would be $488.46 for this level of editing.

Copyediting – CreateSpace describes its Copyediting service as "a professional editor will review your manuscript and give you suggested corrections for grammar, spelling, punctuation, and correct any typos present in the text."

CreateSpace charges $160.00 up to 10,000 words, and $.016 per word over 10,000 words. So, for *I Can't Pay the IRS*, the cost would be $372.16 for this level of editing.

CreateSpace also offers a package deal if you hire them to do both types of editing. You can get their "Editing Package" that includes both types of edits for $300 up to 10,000 words, or $.030 per word over 10,000 words. So, $697.80 for *I Can't Pay the IRS*.

Turnaround times on CreateSpace are generally one to one and one-half weeks.

Final Thoughts on Editing

So, you can see that there are a variety of ways to get your book edited. The cost can run from $0.00 to many hundreds of dollars. So, which editor you select may just depend on your personal access to a good editor and your budget.

But, you MUST have someone other than yourself do the final editing. You're too close to the words to see the mistakes! Let someone else find them for you.

Then, once you've got the book fully edited, it's time to get the interior formatted. This is called typesetting. Let's talk about that now.

CHAPTER 11: CHOOSING A BOOK SIZE AND TYPESETTING/FORMATTING

Once your book is completely edited, it's time to choose the size of the book and the interior design and formatting, also known as typesetting.

Choosing the Perfect Book Size

To determine what size your published book should be, you really need to think about how you're going to use your book. Is it a workbook or a "regular" book for reading?

My first two books were 8.5" x 11" in size. They were workbooks and contained sample letters and forms that the readers could copy and use straight out of the books. So, the 8.5" x 11" format worked great for this.

However, the 8.5" x 11" format is too big for the way that I now use my books and the way that I suggest that you use them. My third book was 6" x 9" and the fourth and fifth books were both 5.5" x 8.5". This book is also 5.5" x 8.5."

I really like the 5.5" x 8.5" size the best for creating Authority, Celebrity and Expertise. However, I think the 6" x 9" size works perfectly well too. It will be a personal preference.

I would look at books of both size and see what appeals to you. The 5.5" x 8.5" is easier to mail. That's the ultimate reason that I went with that size.

Typesetting/Formatting

Once you decide on the size of the book, it's time to start thinking about getting the interior formatted. Remember, we want your book to look just like any book that would sit on a bookstore shelf. One of the quickest ways to make your book look self-published is to have no interior formatting (typesetting).

Typesetting is the process of formatting the interior of your book for publication. It sets the font type and style, the indents and spacing, etc. It's what makes the interior of your book look like a book, rather than just a Word document.

As with editing, you can do this for nothing, or pay a few hundred dollars to get your book typeset.

I've done both. But, I would suggest for your first book that you hire someone else to do the typesetting. It's not THAT expensive, and it will save you a lot of time and hassle if you have someone who knows what they're doing handle this part of the book production.

Do It Yourself

If you're determined to do it yourself, there are many free Word templates available on the internet based on the book size that you've selected. You just need to type "[size] Word book template." So, if you go with a 5.5 x 8.5 book, you would type "5.5 x 8.5 Word book template" and you'll be presented with many different free templates.

CreateSpace also offers a variety of free book templates based on the size of your book. Go to www.createspace.com and search for the free "Interior Templates."

Let Someone Else Do It

To find someone to typeset your book, you should look at Fiverr and Upsource. On Fiverr, you can find people to do this for you ranging from $10 to $200, depending on the size of your book. As always, check the reviews before you hire someone. Upwork will probably cost a bit more.

CreateSpace also offers typesetting services. It has two packages. The first is a "Simple Interior Design." This package uses one of ten preset templates that you select. CreateSpace will then design your book interior based on the template that you select. This service currently costs $249.00

The second package is the Custom Interior service. This allows you to mix and match the templates and to add pictures. If you can't find a template that you like in the Simple Interior package, this may be the way to go. This service currently costs $349.00.

Final Thought on Book Size and Typesetting

Whatever you do, just get going. It won't take long to pick a size for your book. Then, find an interior style that you like and get it done!

Once you have the book size and typesetting done, it's time to create the book cover. Let's talk about that now.

CHAPTER 12: CREATE AN AMAZING BOOK COVER

Now that you've got a handle on the interior of the book, it's time to look at the exterior – the book cover. As I've said many times before, you want your book to look as if it could be sitting on any bookstore's shelf. So, the cover needs to look like this too.

One of the quickest ways to make your book scream "Self-Published!" is to have a poorly designed book cover. I've seen way too many books that suffered from this problem. So, you MUST work to make your book cover amazing.

Now, I want to tell you that I have NO artistic skills whatsoever. My stick figures look like they were drawn by a toddler.

So, of course I don't even attempt to create book covers myself. No one would ever read the book if they saw a cover that I had designed.

But even worse, I can't even give any good general directions to a cover designer to get started. So, that means that you're probably going to have an even easier time getting your book cover done than me.

When I published my first book, I had a local graphic designer create the cover. I thought it looked pretty good and I sold a lot of books with that original design.

However, I eventually starting working with a book wholesaler who was able to get my book into bookstores and libraries across the country. However, they had one condition before they would agree to represent me to all the bookstores and libraries – I had to change the cover.

They put me in contact with a professional cover designer that they worked with. And, he did a complete redo of the book cover. And, you know what? It really looked a lot better.

That was my first lesson in book cover design - get someone who actually understands the concept of book cover design – not just someone who has graphics abilities.

For my second book, I again hired a relatively high-priced cover designer. For the third book, I commissioned a very talented artist to actually paint the cover of my book. It looked amazing, and the original artwork still hangs in my office to promote that book!

Fiverr

I found my original cover designers by trial and error and luck. That's probably not the best way to go. So, for the fourth and fifth books, I decided to hire a designer through Fiverr. And, I think the results were outstanding – and cheap and fast.

To get your book cover completed on Fiverr, just go to www.fiverr.com and enter "book cover design" in the search bar. It's possible to get your book cover designed for $5.00.

But, you'll probably pay more for the back and side cover design, and artwork. I paid approximately $75.00 for each of my last two book covers. That's a small fraction of what I paid for any of my first three book covers.

To choose a designer on Fiverr, you should look through their designs to see if something resonates with you and the design that you have in mind for your book. Then, you pay Fiverr and upload information to the designer.

You can typically make several edits to the proposed design. And, before you know it, you have a beautiful book cover!

99designs

For the cover of this book, I used 99designs.com. I've used 99designs for other projects in the past, including the logo design for Up Your A.C.E!. But, this was the first time that I used 99designs personally for a book cover.

There are other companies that operate like 99designs. So, I encourage you to do your own research. But, this is how 99designs works for creating a book cover.

Once you've logged in to the 99designs site, you click "Launch a Contest" and choose "Book Cover." 99designs will then ask you to pick several cover designs to let designers have a sense of what appeals to you.

Then, it will ask you to pick colors that you would like the designers to consider. Then, it will ask you to provide information about you and your book.

Once you've made it through those initial questions, 99designs will ask you to choose a "Design Package." The packages include Bronze, Silver, Gold and Platinum.

The prices for these packages currently range from $299.00 to $1,199.00. The difference in price reflects the number and quality of the designers who will work on your cover.

You see, designers are submitting their book cover designs to you with the hope that you will choose them. Only the winner – as selected by you – gets the prize. That prize is determined by the package that you select. With a higher package, there's more money for the designer and more interest from better designers.

I chose the "Gold" package for the cover of this book and received 37 different book design proposals. Most of them were very good. But, I ultimately chose the cover that you see on this book. For me, it captured the essence of my message better than any other proposed design. I think it looks amazing!

However, I paid 12 times the cost for the cover of this book as I did for the last two book covers. Is it worth it? Absolutely. But, if money is tight, and you're just trying to get your book done and published as quickly and inexpensively as possible, Fiverr will do just fine!

Things to Think About Before You Hire a Designer

So, before I send you out to get your cover designed, I want to talk about some of the elements that you need to think through. Now, a good cover designer will do this anyway. But, it's good for you to understand what needs to go into this.

For me, the title needs to stand out and pop. I especially want it to look good and easily readable on the internet. Yes, I know that I said that I want you to be able to hand out hard copies and that we're not focusing on doing an eBook. But, much of your marketing and positioning will probably be done on the internet through lead pages and on your website – we'll talk about this more later.

And, you're going to want to use your book in a variety of physical promotional products like your business cards and brochures. So, again, it's important that the title be clear and easily read – even in small pictures of it.

So, the title needs to be in big, easy to read letters. The subtitle should be smaller, but still relatively easy to read.

I like to have an image on the front cover the instantly conveys the message of the book. This is usually the hardest part of the process for me.

Sometimes I have an idea, sometimes I don't. I know what I like, so I know it when I see it.

The front cover should also contain your name. Remember, the point of the book is to establish your ACE. So, start building your ACE on the front cover with your name!

Back Cover

The back cover is EXTREMELY important. As I've suggested many times, the "reader" may not read the book at all. Instead, they may just scan the back cover and see that the information applies to them directly.

Then, if they think that information DOES apply to them, this will lead them to look a little more closely at your book. They may then read the amazing information about the author and get a warm, fuzzy feeling from the photo.

If they're still interested, they may then read the Table of Contents and the Introduction and may skim some parts of the book. If they've done that much, they'll call you because you're the expert and have the answers to their problems.

Read the book. Don't read the book. It doesn't matter. The point is to establish your Authority, Celebrity and Expertise, and establish YOU as the ONLY person that can help them solve their problems.

The elements on the back cover of the book will help your reader decide if your book is for them, and lead them down that path straight to you. And, it's probably the second thing that a potential customer will look at – after the front cover – so you need to make it count!

The back cover should contain 5 elements:

1. Copy – the benefits revealed in the book
2. About the Author
3. Author Photograph
4. ISBN
5. Price

So, let's look at each element and see how they will help you to establish you ACE and sell your product or service.

Copy

Let's talk about copy first. As much as I don't want your book to be a blatant sales letter, it IS vitally important that the book SELL you and your services. The copy on the back of the book is one of those places where you can – and should - ramp up the sales hype.

Unless you have some talent as a copywriter – writing good sales copy - I would suggest that you hire someone to do this for you. I've been getting better at doing this myself, but I've also been studying copywriting for years, and have spent tens of thousands of dollars in the process.

But, I STILL hired a copywriter to help me with the back cover for this book! Yes, it's that important!

Although I think it's important for every professional or business person to understand how to write good sales copy, I don't want you to stress over this if that's not where you are at this point. Remember, we're trying to get your book done – NOW. Let's do whatever it takes to accomplish that. So, that probably means hiring someone to do it for you.

But, before I send you off to my normal sites to hire someone, I'm going to show you my technique for doing book cover copy. You can actually do this yourself. But, you'll still probably get better results if you hire a professional. However, if money is an issue, try this do-it-yourself approach.

I believe that there are 4 things that the back cover copy should contain:

1. A strong headline that makes a promise
2. Easy to read copy
3. An easy, powerful rhythm
4. A focus on features – not benefits

I want people to be able to scan the front of the book, turn it over and immediately know that it is – or isn't – for them.

1. A Strong Headline

For *I Can't Pay the IRS*, the back cover headline is "Wage Garnishments? Bank Levies? Tax Liens? Audit? Problem Solved!"

It's a strong headline and makes a promise. Right? It's really that easy. You can easily use that formula for your own headline. ... Problem? Problem? Problem? Problem? Problem Solved!

Look at the back cover of this book. Is there a strong headline?

2. Easy to Read Copy

For my last several books, I used bullet points to list the benefits of reading the book. I varied from that formula for this book. However, regardless of the format you choose, you want the reader to be able to pick up the book and scan the back copy to quickly get an idea if the book is going to help them solve one or more problems.

3. An Easy, Powerful Rhythm

This one's not as easy to understand. I like short, choppy, to-the-point copy. There's a rhythm to it – and it's easy to read and digest.

If you use bullet points, the rhythm and flow should happen automatically.

4. Focus on Features

When I write copy for the back of my books, I want a prospect to read the back cover and say – "Oh my gosh, that's exactly what I need." "I HAVE to read this book." Good copy should always get into the conversation that's going through your reader's head. You need to know what's keeping them up at night, and give them the answer.

Let me give you an example of what I'm talking about. In my tax resolution business, people usually seek me out when the IRS first starts to do bad things to them – like garnish their wages or their bank account. So, stopping collection activity is one of their primary concerns.

In the copy on the back of the book, the first bullet point says "36 ways to stop IRS collections – immediately!" You can see that this is something that most of my target audience is going to be extremely interested in and will want to read the book to find out how to do this.

(Or, they may just skip the book, identify me as the expert to solve their problems, and call me immediately! Either way works for me!)

Let's look at another of the bullet points. Many big tax resolution companies push settlements with the IRS. They promote this strategy with multimillion dollar radio, television, and pay per click campaigns. So, many consumers are aware of this strategy and want to know more.

So, the next bullet point is about this. "9 steps to slash your tax debt, EVEN if you are in default and facing levies or garnishments and how to negotiate the deal." Notice that I focused on the benefit, not the feature. The benefit is what the reader gets – the feature is what provides it. So, in this case, the feature is the navigating the Offer in

Compromise program. This is the actual program that the IRS offers to settle tax debt.

But, guess what? People don't care HOW you do something, they want the transformation – not the explanation. So, the BENEFIT is the transformation. In this case, it's slashing tax debt. The reader doesn't care about the Offer in Compromise program – the how. They just want their tax debt slashed and they want me to do it.

So, you get the point. And, yes, I actually do go through the book and calculate the number of times the benefit appears in the book. You should do this too.

So, first think about the conversation that's going on in your reader's head. What is keeping them up at night. Then, focus on the transformation that you can offer by focusing on the benefits of your solutions.

Most professionals and business owners tend to think in terms of features – not benefits – and don't really understand the difference and why it's important. So, I'm going to give you an easy way to identify whether something is a feature or a benefit.

All that you have to do is say this sentence … "Here's what this means to you …" If the next statement makes sense, then it's probably a benefit. If it doesn't make sense, then it's probably a feature.

So, for example, I've been an attorney for 26 years. There are certainly places to use this in your ACE positioning, but it's NOT a benefit. Let's use the sentence to see if we can identify this.

"Here's what this means to you. I've been an attorney for 26 years." That may be nice, but it doesn't mean anything. How about this instead.

"Here's what this means to you. I can stop your law suit – dead in its tracks - slash your debt overnight, save your property, and help you get your life back on track - quickly, efficiently, and with minimal interruption, because I've filed 6,000 bankruptcy cases over 27 years and have bankruptcy process down to a smooth science."

OK. I know that's overkill (And, don't yell at me that the Bar would never approve that statement. I'm making a point!)

Let's go back to the Offer in Compromise example and try our sentence. "Here's what this means to you. I'll tell you all about the Offer in Compromise program." What's the reader going to say? "So what?" That's right.

Now, let's try it again. "Here's what this means to you. 9 steps to slash your tax debt, EVEN if you are in default and facing levies or garnishments and how to negotiate the deal." Do you see the difference?

Now, try this with your own copy. Think about the sentence "Here's what this means for you …"

Then, try to think of all the things that are going through your readers' minds about your topic, and what your book is teaching them about that. And, you should be good to go.

Finding a Copywriter

Now, let's say that you DON'T want to do it yourself and are looking to hire someone to write the copy for you. You already know what I'm going to say. You need to look at Fiverr and Upwork.

As I said before, Fiverr will cost less. But, you'll probably find more talented copywriters on Upwork. As always, you'll need to determine your budget to make this decision.

About the Author

The About the Author section is your chance to Up Your ACE! You need to let the reader know that you're the expert to solve their problem. This is the section to do that.

In *I Can't Pay the IRS*, I was listed as "America's Taxpayer Champion". I am because I say I am. In the book before that, I was "America's Homeowner Champion."

You may not want to go that far - or you may. You can anoint yourself anything that you like. You don't need permission or a certification board. So, think about this when you're drafting your About the Author section.

You may be Houston's wildest baker. Or, Denver's Home Restoration Champion. Or, LA's Tooth Whitening Champion. You get the idea. People actually remember this stuff – and accept it!

What market are you trying to reach? Is it local or global? This is the place to target that market.

Next, I again establish my authority with "helping thousands of taxpayers." But, then I tear myself down again.

We talked about that earlier. I want people to know that they can relate to me. Now, that may not always be appropriate for everyone. But, consider this technique. It can be very powerful.

Finally, I get one more shot in at ACE development, then a series of benefits. So, this is a combination of ACE development and benefit pushing.

Take a look at how I did this. Most About the Author sections are full of accomplishments and nothing else. I like to use it for more than that. It's important to establish your ACE in this section. But, you can do so much more.

Author Photograph

It's REALLY important that you have a good – and appropriate - photo of yourself in your book. Will a reader judge a book by its cover? And author photograph? Absolutely.

You MUST have a recent and appropriate photo of yourself on the cover. What does that mean? If you're a professional selling your services, it's appropriate for you to wear a suit and tie like I did in my photograph, or a dress blouse and slacks or a dress if you're a woman.

However, if you're a plumber, it may not be appropriate. You need to think about your target audience and what will establish your ACE.

Also, the photograph MUST NOT be a selfie. I can't tell you how many author photos I've seen on self-published books that are clearly selfies – with low light, crooked angles, etc. If you want your book to look like a book, and to up your ACE, you MUST have a professional photo.

This really means that you need to have a professional photographer take the photo. If you already have one that you use, great. If not, spend a little bit of money and get one made. You can repurpose it over and over.

The ISBN

The ISBN stands for the International Standard Book Number. The ISNB is a unique 13 digit number assigned to every published book. It identifies a title's edition, publisher, and physical properties such as trim size, page count, and binding type. You'll see it as the bar code on the back cover of all books.

That's probably all that you need to know about the actual workings of the ISBN – other than that you need to have one for your book. It's always placed at the bottom right part of the back cover.

There are two ways to get an ISBN for your book. The first is to order one from Bowker. Bowker is the only US company authorized to issue ISBN's. At this time, you can get a single ISBN and a barcode for $150.00. Go to www.bowker.com.

I used Bowker to get the ISBN's for my first three books.

Another alternative, and this is what I've done for the last books, is to let CreateSpace assign an ISBN for you. It's free. That means that you can't sell your book through retailers other than Amazon.

But, I don't think that really matters. We're really not trying to sell books. We're just trying to make our book look like a real book so that you can attract more customers and obliterate the competition! Therefore, you need the ISBN barcode on the back cover of your book to make it look like a book that would sit on a bookstore shelf!

So, don't stress over the ISBN. If you have the money, buy the ISBN. If you're on a tight budget, let CreateSpace assign it for you.

Price

I believe that you should have the retail price of your book listed on the back cover. I know I told you that we are NOT trying to sell books. So, why should it matter if you list a price on the book?

Well, there are two reasons. First, as you know, we want the book to look like a book that would be sitting on a bookstore shelf. ALL books sitting on a bookstore shelf have a price listed on the cover. So, you need one, too.

In addition, you want people to believe that your book has value – even when you give it to them for free. People will appreciate a book more when they think that they would normally pay $19.95 or $24.95 to purchase the book. It sounds crazy, but it's true. So, just trust me on this.

I know the next question. How much should you charge? That's really up to you. However, I would suggest that you stay in the range of prices for similar books.

I typically price my books at $19.95 to $25.95. I would suggest that you do the same. You want to establish a value for the book – so that your reader will value it. But, you also want to be reasonable. Remember, it needs to look like a book.

If you price it at $3.95, the reader won't value it. If you price it at $49.95, the reader won't believe that it's a real price. You get my point.

I would keep the price at between $19.95 and $29.95 – no more, no less.

Final Thoughts on Creating an Amazing Book Cover

I can't emphasize this enough. Your cover – both front and back – must be as good as you can possibly afford. Your potential reader – your prospect or potential referral source – is going to look at the front cover first, and then turn the book over and review the back cover. If you don't grab their attention with the front and back covers, you're done. So, don't let this happen.

There's no point in writing and publishing a book to become the Celebrity in your niche if your book cover repels your Ideal Customer. So, make the cover AMAZING!

Then, once you have an AMAZING book cover, it's time to finally publish the book. I'm going to tell you how to do that now!

CHAPTER 13: HOW TO GET YOUR BOOK PUBLISHED

I've talked about CreateSpace throughout this book. Now, I'm going to show you how to use CreateSpace to publish your book.

There are other options available for self-publishing. But, I'm not going to talk about them. Just use CreateSpace. It will make your life easier.

CreateSpace is owned by Amazon. So, any book that you publish through CreateSpace can be sold through Amazon or through their "Expanded Distribution" option which will allow you to sell to bookstores and libraries.

So, in this chapter, I'm going to tell you everything that you need to know about CreateSpace to get your book published in record time!

Life Before Print on Demand Publishing

But, before we talk about CreateSpace, let's talk about what self-publishing used to look like. When I published my first book, the only way to print books was through a process called "Offset Printing." With this process, you would get a discount based on the number of pages. And, the page count had to be in multiples of 8, 16 or 32.

So, when I created that first book, I ordered 5,000 copies and had them shipped to my house. I waited proudly for that day to arrive. And, then, a giant semi truck pulled up to the house.

The driver looked at my house, and smirked at bit, and then asked me where I wanted the books to go. I first directed him to the garage.

When the garage was completely filled with pallets of books, we started putting them in the living room and then the family room. I even had books in the bedrooms!

Do you know how much space 5,000 book on pallets takes up? A LOT! We lived around those books for a while until we could sell the first batch.

After that, I got smarter. I hired a fulfillment house to store the books in their warehouse, and they shipped the books to bookstores, libraries, the wholesaler, and direct to consumers.

But, all of this convenience had a cost. I had to pay the fulfillment house for monthly storage in their warehouse and to deliver the books. Any savings that I received from printing larger quantities was wiped out by the storage and delivery fees.

Print on Demand Makes It Easy to Publish Your Own Books

I printed and sold a lot of books. But, it was a giant pain! Fortunately for you, we now have Print on Demand – or POD. POD is a beautiful thing and something that you are going to use for your books. You are NOT going to be forced to buy 5,000 copies of your book and then figure out where to store them.

Instead, you'll be able to print small batches – even as low as one at a time – by using CreateSpace's Print on Demand. Yes, it costs more than printing large quantities of books at one time.

But, believe me, and I speak from experience, you should be thankful that we live in an age that makes it profitable to print your books using Print on Demand.

So, let's see how it works.

Open a CreateSpace Account

To start using CreateSpace, you need to open an account. To do this, go to www.CreateSpace.com. Then, click "Start a title for free." Then, "Create a New Account."

Once you get through the New Account creation process, you'll come to the "Start Your New Project" page. Then, just fill in name of your book, select "paperback" for the "type of project" and then select "guided" under the setup process.

CreateSpace will then guide you through the entire setup for your book. It will ask you to upload the interior of your book and the complete cover – front and back - in PDF. Then, CreateSpace will review everything that you uploaded to make sure that your book will print correctly.

Approve the Proof

Once CreateSpace has analyzed your book for errors, it will want you to approve a proof of the book. There are three ways to do this.

First, you can review a virtual digital proof of your book. You can "flip" through the pages and look at everything.

You can also download a PDF of the completed book to view it on your computer. Alternatively, you can print the PDF and see how it looks in the physical world.

Finally, you can have CreateSpace print an actual book and have them mail it to you. Using this method, you can hold the actual physical book in your hand and see how it will REALLY look.

I've done it all ways. Initially, I wanted to hold the book in my hand and make sure that it looked good. So, I ordered the physical copy of the book.

However, for the last several books, I've felt good enough about the process so that I didn't worry about the way the book was going to look. I knew that it was going to look great and appear exactly the way that it looked on the virtual proof review.

And, I didn't want to wait any longer than needed to start printing the actual books. Remember, speed and momentum are your friends. Anything that slows this down stops the momentum. So, now I just review the virtual book. You'll need to make your own choice about this.

Select Your Distribution

Once you have your book proofed, you have a few more things to do. First, CreateSpace wants you to select distribution channels for your book. Here are your choices.

Amazon

You definitely want your book to appear on Amazon. People understand Amazon. If you tell them that your book is available on Amazon, they understand this and will be impressed. It establishes a value for your book – and you'll probably make sales as well.

Amazon Europe

If your book would interest European readers, this option may also make sense for you.

CreateSpace eStore

You can sell your books directly to the reader and still allow Amazon to print and send the book to the reader. You'll make a slightly higher commission by doing this, because you're doing all the marketing and hosting the landing page or website for the ad for the book.

Expanded Distribution Channels:

Bookstores and Online Retailers

This option allows you to potentially get you book into bookstores and other online retailers.

Libraries and Academic Institutions

This option allows you to potentially get your book into libraries.

CreateSpace Direct

This option allows wholesalers to buy larger amounts of your book from CreateSpace and sell them to retailers. You'll make less commission, but who cares. You're NOT trying to make money from royalties. You're trying to get your books to as many of your target audience as possible.

None of these distribution options cost anything, so select them all. It can't hurt. And, it may expand the reach of your book.

Cover Finish

The last part of getting your book finished a printed is to select a cover finish. You can select matte or glossy. I personally prefer the glossy finish. You can order a sample if you wish. Or, just select glossy.

How Much Will it Cost to Print Your Book?

You're probably wondering how much it's going to cost to print each book. Once you've completed everything, CreateSpace will show you the cost for each book. There will also be a charge for shipping the book, depending on where you're located.

For *I Can't Pay the IRS*, at 117 pages, the cost for each book is $2.26. My third book, "*Save Your Florida Home ... Now*! at 309 pages total, costs $4.59 to print each book. So, that might give you an idea of the cost.

If you're going to use your book as a marketing tool - and you should - you'll probably give away most of your books. So, you'll want to keep the cost of this reasonable. As you can see, *Save Your Florida Home ... Now* costs more than twice *I Can't Pay the IRS*. Honestly, *Save Your Florida Home ... Now* is too long for our purposes.

So, I would stick to the moderate size book, like *I Can't Pay the IRS*. It has 107 numbered pages, and 117 total pages.

Final Thought on Getting Your Book Published

If you've followed the steps in this book, getting your book published is going to be easy – and fast. Just upload your files to CreateSpace, add the additional information and get ready to hold your new book! Depending on the shipping options you choose, you could have your printed book in hand in less than one week!

Section 5 – Use Your Book to Become THE Authority, Celebrity and Expert

Congratulations. You've written and published you book! That's amazing. You've joined the ranks of the relatively few who say that they want to write a book – but then actually do write a book.

But, although it's great to be an author, you now need to Up Your ACE by getting the book into the hands of potential clients, customers, referral sources and media outlets. As I've said before, being a published author makes you the Authority and Expert in your niche. You need to PROMOTE your book to now become the Celebrity in your niche.

So, how do you do that?

In this section, we're going to talk about different ways to use your book to become not only THE Authority and Expert in your niche, but also THE Celebrity in your niche. Some of this will be fairly advanced. Some of it will be easy. For now, I want to give you some ideas that you can implement immediately, and other ideas to consider for the future.

CHAPTER 14: EASY-TO-IMPLEMENT GUERILLA MARKETING TECHNIQUES

You can become THE Celebrity in your niche very fast and with little out-of-pocket cost. I've always tried to be efficient with my marketing and promotional dollars. I'll certainly spend money to make money, but I want to make sure that I'm getting a good return for my investment.

That's why I think being a published author is one of the best and most efficient investments you can make in yourself and your business. Hopefully you see now that writing and publishing a book can be quick and inexpensive.

But, if you're short on marketing dollars, you can still become THE Celebrity in your niche by using any number of inexpensive, guerrilla marketing techniques. I continue to use all of these techniques today, even though I have the budget to use other methods. Why? Because they work and the return on my investment is incredible.

So, I encourage you to start with these techniques, even while you're preparing to implement the other techniques that we'll discuss in the next chapters.

Create a Sell Sheet

Something you should consider at the beginning of your efforts to market your book is to create a "Sell Sheet". A sell sheet is just that – a marketing piece that attempts to sell your book.

Now, in my model, I'm not actually trying to sell the book. Instead, I'm trying to "sell" the prospect on ordering a copy of the book – even at no cost.

So, why use a sell sheet? Because it will probably increase the number of people who want to read your book. Let me give you an example.

I sent letters to my clients when I first wrote *I Can't Pay the IRS*. I'm going to talk about this in the next section.

After I created the sell sheet for *I Can't Pay the IRS*, I sent letters to the clients offering a free copy of the book WITH a sell sheet and WITHOUT a sell sheet. Guess which one did better?

That's right, the letter with the sell sheet – by a mile. Why? I think it helps for someone to actually visualize the book.

As you can probably guess, I got my sell sheet created on Fiverr. I paid about $20 total for it. I then subsequently paid a lot more money to have it modified. But, the first version was perfectly fine.

So, think about getting a sell sheet created for your book.

Distribute the Book to Current and Previous Customers and Clients

The VERY first thing that you should do once your book is done is to distribute it to current or previous customers or clients. These people probably already know, like and trust you. So, they will be receptive to the idea of your new book.

And, even if they don't need it themselves, they're likely to share it with friends and family.

I used this technique to launch my tax resolution business. I sent a one-page letter to my current and previous clients. I got MANY new clients from this letter.

And, as you may recall from our earlier discussion about the sell sheet, I dramatically increased the response of people asking for the book by enclosing a sell sheet with the letter.

You'll want to use this technique even if the book topic addresses a completely different niche. So, for example, I created my tax resolution business from scratch. All of my current and past clients were bankruptcy and foreclosure clients. I didn't know if any of them had tax problems. But, the letter produced a LOT of new business for my tax resolution company – from the clients themselves and from their referrals.

Prominently Display Your Book in Your Store or Office

If you have a brick and mortar location, you'll want to prominently display your books there. This seems like a really simple thing to do – but it's REALLY powerful. I've made a LOT of money from just placing books in my office. Why does this work?

Clients come in and say "I didn't know that you did that!"

Clients come in and say "My friend or family member needs that!"

Friends and relatives come in with my client or potential client and say "I need that!"

Makes sure that your staff understands that you WANT to give the book away for free. I had a receptionist who wouldn't let people take the book. She would only let them read it in the office!

This is a book that costs me $2.26 to make, and could potentially produce revenue of $5,000+! It took me forever to convince her that I wasn't crazy for giving the book away.

Point? Make sure that your staff understands that your book is a marketing tool!

Send Your Book to Current and Potential Referral Partners

Referrals are GREAT. They generally come presold on you and typically aren't price sensitive. They already trust you because the person that referred them to you trusts you and they trust that person. It's great.

But, how do you establish and maintain those relationships? One way is to send copies of your book to current and potential referral partners. If you're planning on targeting a large group of potential referral partners, you may want to use the letter and sell sheet approach, rather than just sending the book.

But, if you're planning on being more precise with your targeting, I would send the actual book. There's something about lumpy mail that just works. Normally, your solicitation letter might not make it past the gatekeeper before it winds up in the trash.

But, if you send a book, it WILL get to the intended target. And people HATE to throw away a book.

If your target has ANY interest in what you're offering (through your book), they'll keep the book and pull it out when it's appropriate.

Sometimes, I like to use envelopes that get attention as well, including envelopes that look like they came from Federal Express or UPS. Envelopes that look like priority delivery will get opened and ensure that your new book gets into your potential referral partner's hands.

I've often gone into a referral partner's office or store and found my book sitting front and center in their lobby. That's some incredible free marketing! You'll be a Celebrity before you know it!

Leave Your Book Like a Business Card

One of the craziest things that I've done with my books is to leave them in different places like a business card or brochure. So, for example, I've left my book in dry cleaners, doctors' and dentists' offices, truck repair stores, car washes, etc.

Does that sound crazy to you? Well, it works. I also try to pick the right places to leave the books. I don't just leave them anywhere. I think about my target audience first.

So, for a book about tax resolution, leaving the book at a dry cleaners in the center of downtown that serves all the professionals in the city targets my market – and has produced results.

Leaving the book in a truck repair shop targets truck drivers, who are notorious for having tax problems. You get the idea.

Think about your target market. Where do they congregate? Get a book into that place.

Have Someone Else – Not You – Distribute Your Book

In the last section, I talked about leaving the book at various places that your target market congregates. In the section before that, I talked about sending the book to current and potential referral sources. I have an even better way to do both of those things – have someone do it for you.

I have an incredible husband and wife marketing team that distributes my books for me. They're fearless and will walk into any potential referral partner's place of business and almost always will get my book in the hands of the referral source or multiple copies left at the establishment.

Having someone else do this on your behalf can dramatically increase your Celebrity status! I believe that it cheapens you a little bit when you personally drop by a potential referral with a copy of your book in hand - essentially asking for business.

I get approached by other attorneys, CPA's and other professionals all the time. They drop by the office with their business cards, and sometimes a brochure. They don't have a book or any other evidence of their Authority, Celebrity or Expertise. They say that they'd like to establish a referral relationship with me.

But, do you know what happens? They never make it past the receptionist. If I do see their card or brochure, it means nothing to me. Then, I start this chain reaction thinking.

If they came to the office themselves, that must mean that they have free time. If they have free time, that must mean that they don't have many clients. If they don't have many clients, that must mean that they're not be very good. If they're not very good, I don't want to refer business to them. Do you see what I mean?

Is all of this true? I don't know. But, it doesn't matter because that's what I PERCEIVE.

Remember, I told you at the very beginning of this book that perception is the key – not the truth. So, you'll never get any referrals if your potential referral source, or prospect, perceives that you're not good at what you do.

You can change that perception dramatically by having someone else make the pitch for you. It's something entirely different when SOMEONE ELSE shows up to talk about how great you are and gives them a copy of your book. Do you see the difference?

I have a marketing "team" do this for me. But, you can start with a part-time person. They just need to be fearless!

This is a VERY strong technique. I encourage you to try it!

Use Your Book as a Lead Magnet

Now, let's talk about something that's a little more advanced – Lead Magnets. I use my books extensively as "lead magnets." What's a lead magnet? It's a way to bribe potential clients and customers to get them to give you their contact information. This could be a free report, a video series, a blueprint, etc. Or, in this case, it's your book.

Why is this a little bit advanced? Because, to use it, ideally you should be delivering the book through an autoresponder. An autoresponder is just that. It automatically responds to an inquiry from the prospect for your lead magnet – the book.

I'm sure that you've been part of an autoresponder sequence before. If you've ever requested more information about something, and an email appears almost immediately once you ask for more information – that's an autoresponder. It happens automatically.

There are many different autoresponder programs available, ranging from simple and cheap, to sophisticated and expensive. Starting out, you just want something to get the job done. Remember, speed and momentum are your friends. I don't want you to get bogged down with this.

Probably the easiest way to get this done is to hire someone from Fiverr or Upwork. It won't cost much, and it will be worth it.

Let me show you how this works. For *I Can't Pay the IRS!*, I searched on GoDaddy for a domain name that I liked for the book - www.TheIRSBook.com. I then purchased the domain from GoDaddy for $11.95 for the first year.

I then had a "landing page" created to house the sales information for the book. Think of the landing page as a one-page web site.

Guess where that sales information came from for the landing page? Yep – the back cover copy.

Let's look at this now. Go to www.TheIRSBook.com. This landing page was created using a site called Leadpages. You can see it at www.leadpages.net. (I'm now using a competing program called ClickFunnels for most of my landing pages.)

Once the prospect requests the book, they get a thank you email that generates a PDF copy of the book and asks if the prospect wants a hard copy of the book. That way, I can get a physical address as well.

Why do I want to do all of this? Why not just send a book to everyone who may be a prospect? First, it may get expensive. I only want to send the book to people who are really interested.

Second, I want to be able to continually market to the people who have expressed some interest in the book and the material. Once I have that information, I can start a "drip" email marketing campaign that will constantly send the prospect marketing messages, without any input from me.

I use a software program called Infusionsoft. This would be the program that is sophisticated and expensive. But, once you've learned how to use it, it's a beautiful program. I use Infusionsoft to run most of the marketing for my law firm and for my tax resolution company. What I'm demonstrating here is just one small piece of what it can do.

For example, I'll use Infusionsoft to generate a video series to potential clients, based on the particular legal need that they have. We used to lose people who didn't sign up for an appointment the day they called the office.

No more. We have a 24-hour per day marketer sending out emails and videos until the prospect either hires us or tells us to stop sending information.

But, I digress. There are many other autoresponder programs that you can use to deliver a PDF of your book. These include awebber, (www.awebber.com), and Mailchimp, (www.mailchimp.com). Both of these services will work fine and are much less expensive than Infusionsoft. However, at some point, you may want to consider Infusionsoft or ClickFunnels.

Once you've built out your landing page and autoresponder sequence, you can start to use your book in very interesting ways. For example, I put the book on the back of my business card and use the business card as a lead generation tool. Let's talk about that.

Put a Picture of Your Book on Your Business Card, Brochure and Other Marketing Materials

How many business cards have you seen that show a picture of the author's book on the business card? I know. Not many.

Having the book on your business card, brochure and other marketing materials will do two things. First, it establishes you as THE Authority, Celebrity and Expert because you wrote the book. You don't even need to say anything to people who receive your business card or brochure because your book is prominently displayed. They WILL be impressed and will ask you about your book.

Second, displaying your book on your business card, brochure and other marketing materials will allow you to gather contact information from prospects when they download your book. Just use the technique above to gather the information and use an autoresponder to continually, and automatically, deliver your marketing message.

Your book should also be displayed prominently on your website, on your Facebook page and email signature. You get the point.

As I told you several times earlier, clients, prospects, referral sources and media outlets will perceive that you're THE Authority, Celebrity and Expert on the topic of your book, just because you wrote the book. So, make sure that EVERYONE knows you wrote the book! That means that you display it EVERYWHERE!

Final Thought on Guerilla Marketing Techniques

I hope this chapter has given you inspiration on the many different but inexpensive ways you can promote your book to become THE Celebrity in your niche. I've created businesses from scratch with very little money just by using these techniques. They work and they're powerful. So, start promoting your book NOW! You'll be a Celebrity in your niche in no time!

CHAPTER 15: SPEAKING TO BECOME A CELEBRITY

As a published author, you become THE Authority and Expert in your niche. Then, using any of the techniques we discussed in the last chapter, you can become THE Celebrity in your niche. And, you never even need to talk to anyone, other than prospects. This is great for all the introverted entrepreneurs, professionals and small business owners out there.

But, another way to supercharge your path to becoming THE Celebrity in your niche is to speak to more than one prospect at a time. In the marketing world, we would call this "One-to-Many Selling" rather than "One-to-One Selling." You might call this giving a speech, presentation, seminar, webinar or teleseminar.

The benefits of one-to-many presentations are obvious. You can leverage yourself many times over by speaking to a crowd of prospects or referral sources at one time, rather than one at a time. Would you rather present one sales message to one person or to 10? 30? 50? 100? You get the idea.

And, when people see you on the stage, or giving a webinar, that assume that you're an Authority, Celebrity and Expert in your niche, just because you're giving the presentation. That makes it a lot easier to provide the service or product that your Ideal Customer wants and needs with minimal resistance.

I've made a TON of money for my law firm, my mortgage company, and my tax resolution company by giving one-to-many presentations. If I could only choose ONE thing to market myself and my business and let everything else go, I would choose one-to-many presentations every time.

But, I can already feel a lot of you squirming in your seat just thinking about standing in front of a crowd. For many people, giving a public speech is right up there with walking nude down a public road. I get it.

But, there are ways to get past this fear. And, you can start small. Just hang in there with me.

So, in this chapter, I'm going to show you different ways to become THE Celebrity in your niche with one-to-many presentations, and how to use your new book to supercharge that process.

Start Small

If the thought of speaking to a crowd really terrifies you, just start small. I KNOW that you can talk to clients and prospects now, or you wouldn't be in business. So, it's really not that different to talk to one or two additional clients or prospects at the same time. Right?

So, just start with a few clients or prospects at first. For example, you could invite just a few prospects to your office for an informal question and answer session. Or, you could find a small gathering of people to present your information.

Once you see that there's really no difference between one prospect and three, it gets easier to increase the number of people in your audience. If you feel confident delivering your sales message to one client, there's no reason that you won't be confident in front of three prospects – and then more.

Another option is to start with webinars. With a webinar, you don't need to even see how many people are watching you. You can just give your normal presentation to your computer camera and pretend that you're talking to one prospect. We'll talk more about webinars in a moment.

How Do You Find Groups for Your One-to-Many Presentation?

So, let's say that you're ready to harness the power of one-to-many selling. How do you find the groups that contain your Ideal Customers and referral sources?

If you did your homework from earlier in the book, you should know exactly where your Ideal Customers congregate. For my tax resolution business, I'm looking for consumer and small businesses with tax problems. So, there are many groups that will contain my prospects, including professional groups, small business groups, and trade specific groups.

Just do the same for your Ideal Customer. Find out where they congregate in groups and target those groups for speaking engagements.

You also want to do the same thing for your potential referral sources. I generally focus most of my efforts on acquiring new referral partners. Why? Because I like to be efficient.

If I can get one new referral partner, I may get many new customers from that one referral partner. So, by speaking to groups of potential referral partners, you get the leverage of one-to-many selling to find as many new referral partners as possible, and the power of multiplication by having one referral partner send you several new clients. It's one-to-one selling squared!

If you're still struggling to find groups, try searching in Google for variations of your town, target market, associations and clubs where your Ideal Customer may congregate.

Another option is to search the National Trade & Professional Associations Directory - http://www.associationexecs.com. Although this is a subscription service, you can get a free trial. You may also be able to find a copy of the Directory at your local library.

Using Your Book to Get the Speaking Engagement

Once you've located groups that contain your Ideal Customers or potential referral partners, how do you get those groups to invite you to speak to them? The easiest way to do this is with your book.

Find out who is responsible for booking speakers for the group, and send them a copy of your book and a short description of what you can teach their members. You want to emphasize the benefits that their members will receive from your presentation. You should then follow up with a phone call to that person.

You can reverse that process as well, by calling the person responsible for booking and then following up with a copy of your book. This doesn't need to be complicated – just do it!

As I suggested in the last section, I believe that it's even better to let SOMEONE ELSE make the pitch for you. It will be easier to get speaking engagements if your marketing "team" makes the initial contact with the person responsible for booking speakers.

Have that person or persons talk about your new book and how amazing you are and how much their members will benefit by having you speak at their next meeting. This will be more impressive than if you contact them directly. Celebrities don't book their own gigs!

I've used this method over and over throughout the years and have never failed to get in front of any group that I targeted. But, I'll tell you a secret.

The people in charge of booking speakers can't find enough speakers for their groups! They want you more than you know. So, you can mess up the introduction and probably still get a spot in front of their members!

But, don't do this. Use the power of Celebrity and let your book – and your marketing team – get you that speaking gig!

What Do You Say When You're in Front of the Group?

This chapter is NOT meant to be a course on how to give a presentation. However, in general, your presentation will depend on a number of factors, including how long you have to give the presentation. A one-minute presentation will be very different from a 60-minute presentation.

At a minimum, you need to present the problem that your Ideal Customer is trying to solve, teach at least one way that your service or product will solve that problem, and show the ultimate transformation that your Ideal Customer will achieve with your help. This really could be as simple as giving a normal sales presentation that you would give to your Ideal Customer if they were sitting in front of you. It just depends.

Ultimately, your presentation should encourage prospects or referral sources to contact you for additional information about this process. I've found that the best way to do this is to offer copies of my book to the audience.

Depending on the size of the audience, I either give actual copies of my book to everyone in attendance, or I offer them the opportunity to get it for free if they give me their contact information. For large groups, the best way to gather this information is to have them text a number that you have already selected that will send them a PDF copy of the book by autoresponder. This is a variation of the autoresponder model that we discussed earlier.

During a presentation, I make frequent references to my book to emphasize my Authority, Celebrity and Expertise and to encourage them to refer to the book for additional guidance. I also make sure that the audience has several easy ways to reach me for more information.

In addition, I always have a PowerPoint slide that contains a picture of the book and explain how they or their friends or family can get additional copies of the book. Overkill? Nope. It's Celebrity!

Webinars

As I mentioned earlier, webinars can be a good way for you to get comfortable with public speaking before you start speaking to live, in-person groups. And, webinars can be a great ongoing source of new clients, referral sources and income.

Again, this chapter is NOT intended to teach you how to start and run a webinar. I'll share some resources at the end of this chapter for that. For now, I just want to show you how to use your new book to attract people to your webinar, to get people to trust you, and to make more income.

How to Attract Ideal Customers and Referral Sources to Your Webinar

I use my books as bait to get prospects and referral sources to attend my webinars. This accomplishes two things. First, it gets people to self-identify with the topic. Only people who are interested in my book and webinar will register for the webinar. So, I'll only be addressing qualified prospects or referral sources.

Sure, I could get this same effect just by promoting the webinar. But, that's where the second benefit appears – I'm the Authority, Celebrity and Expert on the topic because I wrote the book.

By presenting the webinar, I do get a boost as a Celebrity. But, people are becoming more accustomed to webinars. As the technology has become easier to use, more and more professionals and small business owners are presenting webinars – usually with a sales pitch at the end. So, I've seen more skepticism from webinar audiences now than in the past.

This means that you need to get your audience to not think of you as a salesperson, but as a Celebrity. The best way to do this is to promote your book to them as part of your webinar.

But, how do you do this? I use a variety of techniques to attract people to my webinars. It really depends on the audience that I'm trying to attract. Generally, however, I use direct mail, email and Facebook ads.

If I have, or can get, a list of prospects or referral sources, I will generally promote my book and webinar by direct mail and email. This is pretty straightforward. I generally describe the problem, talk in general terms about a solution, and play up the ultimate transformation that will happen after attending my webinar.

Many of my clients are embarrassed about their problems and aren't ready to talk to someone yet about a solution. But, they can watch a webinar in the comfort – and privacy – of their home and see how I can provide a solution that will give them the ultimate transformation that they're looking for.

You want to make it as easy as possible for your Ideal Customers. And, a webinar is often just the thing to get your Ideal Customer to make a first step. During the webinar, they'll see and hear you in action and feel comfortable that you're THE Authority, Celebrity and Expert to solve their problem – because you wrote the book on it!

As with live presentations, I refer to my book frequently during the presentation, and have at least one PowerPoint slide that highlights the book. I usually offer the book as a bonus for people who stay until the end of the webinar.

Of course, I would give them the book anyway. But, they don't know that!

Final Thoughts on Speaking to Become a Celebrity – and Resources

I encourage you to use a mix of webinars and seminars to promote your Authority, Celebrity and Expertise, and your services and products. They key is to just get moving. Just do it!

If you want to become a better speaker, I encourage you to find a mentor. I've been blessed with many amazing mentors on my journey, and I hired several of them specifically to help me give better presentations. I've also spent a LOT of money in this quest. But, it's been worth every penny.

You can dramatically increase your Celebrity, and your income, by learning to give effective one-to-many presentations. So, I encourage you to sharpen your abilities in this area.

There are many coaches and groups that offer speaker training. But, I can only speak to the ones that I've experienced personally. You can't go wrong with anyone on this list, and I'm presenting them in order of when I trained with them. If you're interested, make sure that you include these amazing trainers on your list:

Joel Bauer – www.JoelBauer.com. Joel is a former magician, turned trade show pitch man, turned mentor to the mentors. He's a master of persuasion, with a soft inner core. Much of who I am as a speaker came directly from Joel.

Dave Dee – www.davedee.com. Dave started as a mentalist, and now teaches students his psychic mind control technics. He's an amazing marketer and a master of one-to-many selling. I've sharpened my sales messages and presentations with his help.

Suzanne Evans and Larry Winget – www.suzanneevanscoaching.org and www.beaspeaker.org. Suzanne is a New York Times Best-Selling author and went from secretary to six million dollar business in six years. Larry Winget is a six-times New York Times/Wall Street Journal Best-Selling author and earns a huge income delivering keynote speeches. Together, Suzanne and Larry offer a balanced approach to speaker training – Suzanne teaches one-to-many selling from the stage, and Larry teaches how to deliver keynote speeches. Their in-your-face style is refreshing and has helped me to sharpen my message and delivery.

Russell Brunson – www.russellbrunson.com and www.perfectwebinarsecrets.com. Although I haven't yet trained live with Russell Brunson, I've used many of his programs and tools. I mentioned one of those tools earlier – ClickFunnels. I've placed him in this section because you should look at his Perfect Webinar program when creating your webinar and seminars. I used this program to create my last several webinars and also to create my stage presentations. Do yourself a favor and purchase the upsell PowerPoint and Keynote slides.

Eric Lofholm – www.ericlofholm.com. Eric is a master sales trainer and has helped me to create a more effective sales message in my presentations – including better ways to close the deal at the end of the presentation.

CHAPTER 16: TRADITIONAL MARKETING

The next three chapters are going to be quick. I just want to introduce you to the concepts and hope that you will explore them as you go.

First, let's talk about what I call traditional marketing. By that, I mean the marketing that we used to do before social media, including direct mail, space ads, newsletters, etc. I also mean the marketing that too many people have started to ignore in favor of social media. There is still a huge place for traditional marketing in your business!

I told you at the beginning of this book that I transformed my struggling law practice by sending a direct mail letter to prospects in which I mentioned my first book in the PS. The letter itself was good. But, it had MUCH more impact because I was a published author.

The Authority, Celebrity and Expertise of the book made that letter – and me – stand out from all the other attorneys who were sending letters to those same prospects. Since that day, ALL of my marketing mentions my books. You should do this as well.

If you use direct mail, and you should, make sure that all of your marketing pieces highlight your book. Make sure that your direct mail letters are amazing on their own. But, you'll increase the response exponentially by mentioning your book.

(If you don't believe me, test it. Send one letter that highlights your book to half of your mailing and send the same letter without mentioning your book to the second half of that list and see which one works better. I already know the answer.)

You should do the same thing for any other traditional marketing that you do. Do you mail a newsletter? Make sure that your book is highlighted in every edition. I would also include a way for people to download the book for free by using the autoresponder technique we discussed earlier.

Do you use space ads? Again, highlight your book. If possible, I would again allow prospects a way to download your book for free and start marketing to them with an autoresponder.

You should do this for EVERY form of marketing that you do. Remember, the WHOLE point of writing and publishing your book is to position you as THE Celebrity in your niche and to stand out from the crowd. It WILL do that if you let it. So, don't hide your book from your Ideal Customers. Highlight it and mention it every chance you get.

CHAPTER 17: TRADITIONAL MEDIA

One of the fastest ways to increase your Celebrity is to get interviews with traditional media, including television, radio and newspapers. And, one of the easiest ways to do this is by using your book to demonstrate your Authority and Expertise.

Just like we discussed for getting speaking gigs, reporters NEED to get stories and are looking for you. They don't want to promote your book, but they ARE looking for experts with interesting stories to tell their readers and listeners.

Appearing on traditional media is one of the quickest ways to catapult your Celebrity within your niche. When paired with your book, appearances on traditional media provide a strong one-two punch!

So, how do you get reporters to interview you? There are two ways – hire a Public Relations company or do it yourself. I've done both.

Do It Yourself Public Relations

For getting on local media, you can probably do it yourself. As before, find out who is responsible for the topic you wish to discuss. Then, reach out to them with your book and a telephone call.

But, reporters and producers are looking for interesting story angles. They are NOT looking to promote your book. So, don't approach them with "Hey, I just wrote this great book. You should interview me about it." You probably won't even get a response to a pitch like this.

However, let's say that you're a dentist that wants to promote your teeth whitening business – and you just wrote the book on teeth whitening. Maybe the story angle that you pitch is that nine out of ten teeth whitening products are harming your teeth and should never be used. (I just made that up.) But, you get the idea. Whatever you do, you need an interesting story angle.

You can't JUST talk about your new book. However, you MUST use the book to establish your Authority, Celebrity and Expertise so that the media outlet feels confident that what you're saying is true.

There's a lot more to this process. But, that's the basic idea. There are multiple products and courses that will teach you to approach traditional media outlets without using a PR company.

Hire a Public Relations Company

However, if you want more interviews, in a shorter period of time, with higher quality media, it probably makes sense to hire a PR company. When I retained PR companies in the past, they were able to quickly book me with radio, television and newspaper outlets across the country.

As a result, I quickly became a Celebrity in my niche. Then, because I had appeared on several major media shows, including national shows, it was even easier to book more appearances. You can do this as well.

However, if you are uncomfortable in front of a camera or microphone, get some practice before you try to swing for the big-time shows. It's better to look or sound stiff and stilted on local shows with smaller audiences, rather than doing that before a national audience!

Pay-to-Play Radio Shows

Another way to establish your Authority, Celebrity and Expertise in your local market is to "sponsor" a radio show. Many radio stations, especially talk radio stations, allow people to host their own radio show. The station charges the host for the opportunity, typically under a contract for a specified time.

Many hosts then charge advertisers for ad spots during their show to offset some or all of the cost of the show. Some hosts also allow guest appearances by local experts and charge the guests for the appearance.

I've appeared on many of these pay-to-play radio shows over the years. I once co-hosted a show with another professional. We each paid half of the $5,000.00 monthly cost for the show, and we shared the time during the hour. I've also appeared for a fee on other shows and for no fee on others.

Most listeners don't realize – or don't care – that the host and guests are actually paying to be on the show. They just assume that the person on the radio must be an Authority, Celebrity and Expert – because they're on the show.

Appearing on local pay-to-play radio shows, either as a host or guest, has been a very inexpensive way to establish me as THE Authority, Celebrity and Expert in my niches. And, of course, I always highlight my books, or make sure that the host does it for me. I also make it easy for people to download my book – using the autoresponder technique that we discussed earlier.

If you haven't appeared on local radio before, take a look at the pay-to-play options in your area. Find a show that caters to your Ideal Client, and reach out to the host or producer about the options for appearing on the show. Then, make sure that you highlight your book during the show and make it easy for your Ideal Customers to get the book!

Final Thoughts on Traditional Media

At some point, and hopefully soon, you should try to get interviews on traditional media. There's probably no faster way to promote your Celebrity status that this. I encourage you to research the books and programs that will show you the best way to do this on your own.

If you have the resources, you may want to find a local PR firm who can get your started in your local area. As you become more comfortable with media interviews, and your Celebrity status increases, it may make sense to approach PR firms with a national presence.

But, for most of us, it's OK to be a big fish in a little pond. That means that being THE Celebrity in your local geographic area is enough. So, you may never need any more media exposure than your local market. And, you can get that exposure from local media and pay-to-play radio stations.

CHAPTER 18: SOCIAL MEDIA

This chapter is going to be short, because I am not a master of social media. However, marketing is marketing. You can improve ALL of your marketing, including social media, by highlighting your book.

You MUST highlight your book in everything that you do, including Facebook, LinkedIn, Twitter, YouTube, etc.

Your Facebook page should contain a picture of your book - and a way to download it. Same for your LinkedIn profile. You get the point.

You will dramatically improve the response of ALL your marketing, including through social media, by establishing your Authority, Celebrity and Expertise with your book. Because you're a published author, you're not just another person with a platform – you're a Celebrity with the Authority and Expertise to validate your comments, opinions and information.

CONCLUSION

I hope that you've enjoyed this journey down the red carpet with me. I hope that your eyes are tired from all the flashing lights of the paparazzi. I hope that you have so many clients chasing you that you need your own security detail to push them back!

If you're not there yet, just remember to follow my simple formula for success:

1. Pick a niche to dominate;
2. Write a book to become the Authority and Expert in that niche;
3. Promote the book to become THE Celebrity in that niche;
4. Watch the money roll in.

And, before I leave you, I want to remind you of why this simple formula works. It's the Secret of Celebrity:

You make more money for WHO you are, rather than WHAT you do!

If you follow the steps in this book, you will be able to write, publish and promote your own book and become THE Celebrity in your niche.

But, if you want to write and publish your own book – FAST – I encourage you to explore the options to work directly with me. For more information, go to www.UpYourACE.com, or call 1-833-IM AN ACE (833-462-6223).

Publishing Hacks is an online premium training program that will help you to quickly and easily write and publish your book. Short, step-by-step video lessons, worksheets, PDF's, outlines and templates will make writing and publishing your book fast, efficient and painless. Just fill in the worksheets and templates as you go, and your book will practically write itself!

I also offer a live, three-day event where a small group of students complete their entire book during the event with my direct help. There's no faster way to complete your book!

The FIRST step to becoming THE Authority, Celebrity and Expert is to become a published author. But, there are more advanced techniques that will take you from Celebrity to Superstar! With my ongoing monthly training program, you'll learn these new techniques.

Finally, I occasionally accept personal clients for private coaching and also conduct small mastermind groups. If you really want to Up Your A.C.E. and explode your income, this may be an option for you.

Whatever path you choose, I hope that I have been a good tour guide! I wish you a good journey down the red carpet to success!

-- Charlie Price

Made in the USA
Columbia, SC
15 November 2017